Meat
in Due
Season

**A Devotional Guide to
Surviving the Storms of Life**

Dr. Victor A. Kennedy, Ph.D.

WESTBOW
PRESS®
A DIVISION OF THOMAS NELSON
& ZONDERVAN

Scripture taken from the King James Version of the Bible.

WestBow Press books may be ordered through booksellers or by contacting:

WestBow Press
A Division of Thomas Nelson & Zondervan
1663 Liberty Drive
Bloomington, IN 47403
www.westbowpress.com
1 (866) 928-1240

ISBN: 978-1-9736-1141-7 (sc)
ISBN: 978-1-9736-1140-0 (hc)
ISBN: 978-1-9736-1142-4 (e)

Library of Congress Control Number: 2017919387

Print information available on the last page.

WestBow Press rev. date: 12/22/2017

$\mathscr{A}$CKNOWLEDGEMENT

I wish to give all the glory to the writing and completing of this book to Jesus Christ. HE is the author and finisher of my faith. Jesus saved me in 1993. HE has been my peace through the many storms of life. I am so grateful for HIS promise of eternal life, and equally grateful for HIS divine presence in my life. Life is frankly better with Jesus than without HIM. Jeremiah 33:3 says…Call unto me and I will answer thee, and show thee great and mighty things thou knowest not.

What about you today? Do you know Jesus? Do you have forgiveness of your sins? Do you know that your name is written in the Lamb's Book of Life? If you have not surrendered your life to Jesus Christ, I encourage you to give your life to HIM today. HE promised in Isaiah 55th Chapter to abundantly pardon us if we ask. A pardon in Christ Jesus takes away the guilt and judgement of our sinful acts. I am so glad to have been pardoned through the Blood of Jesus. This is why I love to tell people about Jesus, and HIS glorious salvation.

We have great and precious promises in Jesus. I hold to the promise of seeing those who died in Christ again in Heaven. I hold to the promise that I am saved and forgiven. I forgive others out of gratitude for Jesus lovingly forgiving me. Please look at John 3:1-7, John 3:15-18, John 14:1-9. Acts 2:37-42, Romans 3:23, Romans 6:23, Ephesians 2:8-9, and Revelation 20:10-15. There are so many wonderful verses in God's Word, that show the goodness, joy, and peace in Christ.

HE has blessed me mightily, and gave me the motivation to write this book. I pray that these 104 devotional messages greatly bless and encourage you. I also pray that all who read this will know the awesome love and forgiveness of Jesus Christ.

God Bless.
Dr. Victor A. "Vic" Kennedy, Ph.D.

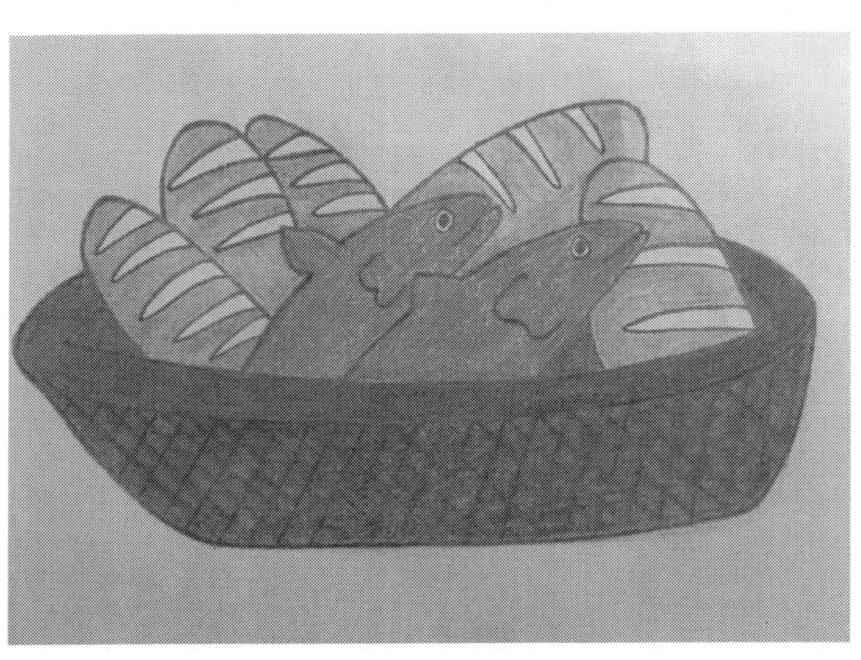

# ONE

28 Come unto me, all ye that labour and are heavy laden, and I will give you rest.

Matthew 11 :28

Are you in need of rest today? All of us at holiday times are thinking about a little rest. Then we continue life and never truly rest. Jesus said that He will give you rest. He said Matthew 11:28-30... learn of Him. He is meek and lowly of heart. You will find rest for your Soul. When my Soul has rest...I HAVE PEACE!! Peace and rest does not mean that there are no problems. To the contrary, we will have tribulations, but peace does come...after you surrender your life to Him and ask Him to forgive you...He truly does. You are now entering into His rest. I do not labor in Jesus to earn my salvation... I labor because I have His Salvation, and in love and gratitude, I tell the lost world about Him. Even in laboring...I am still at rest. I am at rest, because I learn of Jesus, through His Word...and have His peace in life's many storms. In Philippians 4: 4-9...the Apostle Paul wrote... Rejoice in the Lord always, again I say rejoice. In verse 6, he said don't worry. In verse 7...He said God will give you the peace (rest) that passes all understanding. Paul wrote that from a Roman prison. David fled from King Saul, and from a cave penned Psalm 34...he rejoiced in God's deliverance. The prophet ISAIAH wrote in Ch. 26:3... God will keep you in perfect peace, IF you keep your mind stayed on Him. Assyria was giving Judah a fit...yet he had peace. We NEED to turn everything in our lives over to Jesus. He is King of Kings, but also the Prince of Peace.

Today...let's all surrender to Jesus. Take on His peace, and find rest for our souls... God bless.

# Two

103 How sweet are thy words unto my taste! yea, sweeter than honey to my mouth!

Psalms 119 :103

There is nothing sweeter or better than the Word of God. A week ago, Jesus truly touched my heart with sweetness of His Word. His Word has moved me to a deep place of worship. His Words are a lamp unto my feet, and a light unto my path... Psalm 119: 105. Consider what you are going through right now...It may be a hard and bitter trial. There is nothing sweeter than the Word of God in the midst of a tough situation. Psalm 34:8 says... O taste and see that the Lord is good, blessed is the man that trusteth in Him. We see with our eyes, yet the Word of God says...taste and SEE. Once you put the Word of God in your heart, trust Him, and speak His Word... hope comes to hopeless situations. Victory comes out of despair. Here is a big one... Love comes out of hate. That is what the sweetness of the Word of God can do. Titus 1:2 says... God cannot lie. His Word is true. His Words calmed the storm in Mark 4. His Words raised Lazarus from the dead in John 11. His sweet Words brought me from death to life, when He promised to forgive me in Proverbs 28:13 and 1st John 1:9, if I would confess my sins; He did it. I am forgiven, and it doesn't get sweeter than that!! That's why I know it is right to be quick to forgive all offenses leveled at us. The sweet promise of Jesus love, mercy, and help in the time of trouble, changes the way we walk, talk and think. I am no longer defeated. I have a loving Savior, who gave me the sweetness of His Word, grace, mercy. and eternal life for His children.

Today...taste and see that the Lord is good. Trust Him and be blessed, and enjoy the sweetness of His Word... God bless.

$\mathcal{T}$HREE

26 A new heart also will I give you, and a new spirit will I put within you: and I will take away the stony heart out of your flesh, and I will give you an heart of flesh.

Ezekiel 36 :26

Time for open heart surgery. Ezekiel was a mighty prophet, speaking to Israel in a very difficult time. He was used by God to tell the people that a change was coming in how God was going to relate to them. He was going to put His Spirit within us, and change us from the inside. I was in service Sunday, and a powerful Word was preached, telling us from Isaiah 43 and John 15 and 1st Peter 2:9, that we were chosen by the Lord Himself, before the foundation of the world. You are reading this because none of us are perfect, completely changed, and walking on streets paved with gold yet. 1st John 4: 18 says perfect love casts out fear. Hearing Sundays message showed me that we need perfect love...not there yet. I needed some open-heart surgery, that comes from God's Word. I found myself weeping and seeking a deeper relationship with such a loving Savior. Jesus wants all of us to strive and press toward the high calling of God in Christ Jesus (Philippians 3:14). We can all check ourselves... Galatians 5:22-24...are we walking in the fruit of the Spirit... love, joy, peace, etc. No? Open heart surgery needed. Do we forgive like it NEVER HAPPENED? No? That's Mark 11:25-26 again. If we don't... open heart surgery is needed. Do I really, truly love like Jesus? No? Then open heart surgery is needed!! Jesus said in Revelation 3: 20... Behold, I stand at the door and knock...why is He on the outside? Because that heart of stone is keeping Him out. He got my attention Sunday...He must increase, I must decrease.

Today...Please let Jesus perform His surgery on your heart...let Him have His way in your life... God bless.

FOUR

60 And He kneeled down, and cried with a loud voice, Lord, lay not this sin to their charge. And when He had said this, He fell asleep.

Acts 7 :60

This is the definition of love, mercy, grace and true forgiveness. In the 7th chapter of Acts, Stephen was brought before the elders in Jerusalem. He was a man of God...filled with His Spirit, and doing good works. He preached a powerful message to the Pharisees. He laid out their entire history, and in the end... called them prideful and disobedient to the Word of God. Stephen told them in Acts 7: 51-53...he told them that they were wrong, and were the children of the men that had killed the prophets. Acts 7: 54 says... when they heard this, they were cut to the heart...they became so angry that they grabbed him, and cast him out of the city. Keep in mind that they were all Jewish brothers, and subject to the same Word of God, that told them to love their brother. They then stoned Stephen. Stoning meant hurling huge rocks at him, and smashing in his body and head. A Pharisee named Saul of Tarsus held the garments of them who did the stoning. Saul of Tarsus cheered them on as they killed Stephen. Stephen looked into Heaven and saw Jesus... STANDING... not sitting on the throne. When they touched Stephen... Jesus stood up for His child. After seeing the nail scarred hands of Jesus, and seeing His Glory, Stephen said...Lord lay not this sin to their charge...in other words... forgive them. After seeing Jesus, all Stephen could do is forgive. Saul of Tarsus was set free of that sin, and put in a spiritual place where Jesus could save him. Read Acts 9th chapter; Saul of Tarsus...killer and persecutor of the Church... became the Apostle Paul... Jesus' greatest soul winner. All possible because of a man named Stephen, who forgave.

Today...Let us truly love and completely forgive...God bless.

$\mathscr{F}$IVE

1 Blessed is He whose transgression is forgiven, whose sin is covered.

Psalms 32 :1

This is an awesome blessing...one we ALL need. This message is staying in last week's theme about forgiveness. The power and love of Jesus is so mighty to forgive our sins. David had sinned, and when Nathan the prophet spoke to him, he did what we should do when we recognize our wrongdoing. David said... I have sinned against the Lord. Nathan essentially told him that he was forgiven. There was no hesitation. David repented...he was forgiven. He penned Psalm 32 and 51 when he realized how much mercy he had been given. Why could David get mercy for his sin. When his mentor and father in law King Saul tried to kill him, David refused to put his hand against Saul. David sowed mercy, and was able to reap mercy (read Galatians 6:7-10... sowing and reaping). David's sin was covered, and he was not removed from the throne. He was forgiven. The new testament takes our forgiveness promise even higher. Because of Jesus dying on the cross for our sins... taking our punishment on himself...our sins are not just covered, but washed away and removed from the sight of God completely. Not covered...washed away. When the Apostle Paul was baptized in Jesus name...Ananias said to him in Acts 22:16...arise...wash away thy sins... calling on the name of the Lord. The many evil things that Saul of Tarsus did to the church were washed away... he became the Apostle Paul. Stephen forgave and look at the result. He was being stoned to death...then an amazing thing happened...Agape love and forgiveness. Saul of Tarsus stood by cheering those who were stoning Stephen. Stephen forgave them before he died. Saul of Tarsus became the Apostle Paul soon after. Real forgiveness is deep. It is what Jesus does for us... we must forgive like that too.

Today... Let us remember...Blessed are the forgiven, who forgive also... God bless.

SIX

6 Be strong and of a good courage, fear not, nor be afraid of them:
for the LORD thy God, He it is that doth go with thee; He will not
fail thee, nor forsake thee.

Deuteronomy 31 :6

Today we are walking this message together. This scripture in Deuteronomy is also echoed in the New Testament in Hebrews 13:5... I will never leave you nor forsake you. No theology... just truth. I have been saved in Jesus Christ for 24 years. Jesus has kept me. I can't say that I know that Jesus is true to His Word, unless I have been in a place where it is easy to feel forsaken. When you want to throw in the towel...turn to Jesus, the author and finisher of our faith (Hebrews 12:1-2). An old King David wrote it Psalm 37... I was young, now am old, yet have I not seen the righteous forsaken nor his seed begging bread. David had everything taken in 1st Samuel 30...He encouraged himself in the Lord. He was told... pursue... you shall recover all. The A part is that he encouraged himself in the Lord. I am blessed to have brethren in the Lord, who believe with me. At the time of trouble, we can touch and agree in prayer...ask Jesus for strength. He answers back...Be of good courage...wait on me... I will not leave you nor forsake you. Even when Jesus was praying in the Garden of Gethsemane, prior to being crucified... heavenly help was sent. Jesus was sweating blood in the stress of His prayer, knowing what He was going to face. An angel was dispatched to help Him. Jesus went through His disciples leaving Him, and the crowd turning on Him. He has been there, and understands. Jesus gave us a promise here, and cannot lie.

Today, I choose to receive the encouragement that I need. Please reach out to Jesus, and take the encouragement that you need, knowing He will never leave you nor forsake you... God bless.

_SEVEN

22 It is of the LORD's mercies that we are not consumed, because his compassions fail not.

Lamentations 3 :22

Where would we be without His mercy? Without the mercy of Jesus...we would have no hope. Mercy is when we do not get we do deserve (Romans 3:23... For all have sinned). Then there is grace (God's unmerited favor). Grace is us receiving what we don't deserve. John Chapter 1:1-17 tells us that that grace and truth came by Jesus Christ. When Jesus said from the cross..."Father forgive them for they know not what they do"...we were given mercy. His mercy is new every day. Romans 6:23 reminds us that the wages of our sin is death. Jesus came to the rescue, with His gift of mercy and forgiveness and salvation. Without His mercy...we would be done... consumed... with no hope. This is why I love Jesus so much. We owed a debt that we could not pay... Jesus paid a debt that He did not owe. This seems like such a basic message here... but it is the one that unfortunately keeps being missed. We are not consumed and get His new mercy daily. Jesus said in Matthew 7:2, that with the same judgement we measure out, will be measured back to us. I have previously quoted Mark 11:25-26 in no less than 10 previous devotions. Jesus said...if we don't forgive...we are not forgiven. WHY?? Because if I don't measure out the same mercy and forgiveness given to me, I forfeit that mercy. Without the mercy of Jesus Christ, we are doomed to be consumed. Yet according to 1st John 4:19...He loved us first!! Jesus targeted you and I for His love and mercy, even when we weren't thinking about Him.

Today, let us all remember that Jesus was merciful with us, never take that for granted, and extend that love, grace and mercy to one another... God bless.

IGHT

67 Before I was afflicted I went astray: but now have I kept thy word.

Psalms 119 :67

How do I really get to know Jesus? Recently, we looked at Job 13:15... Though He slay me yet will I trust Him... Psalm 34 was written while David was fleeing from 2 enemies. He said... Many are the afflictions of the righteous, but the Lord delivereth him out of them all. If you read Psalm 119:67, 71and 75... you see a recurring theme that lined up with Job, and Psalm 34... I would never had learned the ways of God without trials and tribulations. I would have no faith, if I had never been tried in who and what I believe. I know that Jeremiah 33:3 is true because I was put in tough situations. That verse reads...Call unto me and I will answer thee, and show thee great and mighty things that thou knowest not. I would not know that Jesus could do miracles, change my heart and mind, or fix what is unfixable, if I had never been in a place where I really needed God to do it. In fact, if you and I are honest, we did not come to Jesus when all was well. He had to rock the boat in our lives, so that we would say...Yes Lord. Sometimes we keep Jesus at arm's length, until He shakes things up. Verse 67 is true... before I was afflicted I went astray... I did life my way. Please hear me today, if His affliction brings you to Jesus, or keeps you in Jesus, or brings you back to Jesus...it is a good thing. Whether we believe it or not... through the troubles, you have just experienced His love. Now we know that we can trust Him in all things, and know that through the troubles...He is growing and refining us.

Today...know that the troubles are tough, they do not feel good... but in the end with Jesus...we win. God bless.

$\mathcal{N}$INE

15 Though He slay me, yet will I trust in him: but I will maintain mine own ways before him.

Job 13 :15

Staying true through adversity. Job was a man whom the Word of God declared to be a good man, who truly feared and loved God. He went through a terrible trial, where it appeared that all was lost. Through the toughest trial, comes the greatest victory. James 1st chapter says... Blessed is the man who endures temptation...He shall receive the Crown of Life. 1st Peter 4:12 says... Beloved think it not strange concerning the firey trial which is to try you, as though some strange thing happened unto you. The next verse tells us to REJOICE!! I am writing this during the Passover (and the celebration of Our Lord's resurrection) ...a time when Jesus shows Himself mighty. We just celebrated His resurrection...the greatest Passover victory of all. Yes...the warfare is great, but your victory will be great. Though we are going through... Though He slay me...yet will I trust Him. I have gotten to know Jesus Christ through adversity. Every time I believe that I have learned how much He can keep me, or strengthen me, or deliver me, He allows me to have a deeper situation, to get to know my Lord better. What is coming for you and I if we hang on to His nail scarred hand...The Crown of Life...The Crown of Glory, and a trust in Jesus that we could only have learned through trials.

Today...let's all truly trust Jesus now and always... let's pray one for another... no matter the trial... God bless

$\mathcal{T}$EN

25 I, even I, am He that blotteth out thy transgressions for mine own sake, and will not remember thy sins.

Isaiah 43 :25

This is why Hebrews 10:25 is so important. That is the verse that tells us not to miss fellowship in church. While sitting in church, I heard from the Lord to send this out. This is the Passover season. At Passover, the blood of a lamb was placed above the door and lentil of the homes of the Hebrew slaves in Egypt. God had hardened the heart of Pharaoh to get His judgement on him (this is why a hard heart is so dangerously unprofitable). The slaves were going to be set free, and the death angel was going to take the firstborn of Egypt. Those who had the blood of the lamb applied would be passed over. Miracles are done at Passover... like the walls Jericho coming down, or Peter's rescue from prison. The miracle of the first Passover was the death angel passing over, and Israel going free. The miracle of Passover in 33 A.D. was that while the Passover lamb was being slain in the Temple, Jesus...the Lamb of God was dying on the cross of Calvary, so that we could be truly free, have our sins blotted out, and remembered no more!! What a Passover miracle. This scripture lines up with Psalm 103 and Hebrews 8th chapter, where he promised to hear our repentance and remember our sins no more. Revelation 20: 10-15 reminds us that there is a Book of Life for those who say yes to Jesus, repent of their sins and acknowledge His Lordship. There are the Books of Remembrance for those who reject the sacrifice of Jesus... the Passover Lamb.

Today...know that Jesus is the Lamb of God, who takes away the sin of the world. When we repent, He is there to blot out what we did from the Books of Remembrance, and to put our names into the Book of Life. Remember when you are forgiven, you must forgive. Thank you, Jesus, for your sacrifice... God bless.

$\mathcal{E}$LEVEN

5 But He was wounded for our transgressions, He was bruised for our iniquities: the chastisement of our peace was upon him; and with his stripes we are healed.

Isaiah 53 :5

This is a good reason to love Jesus so much. This is one of the 355 prophecies of Jesus Christ. These were written hundreds, in some cases thousands of years before His birth. Isaiah 53:5 says that Jesus was wounded for our sins and wrongdoing. He was bruised for the iniquity of us all. The 39 lashes that He took across His back were for our healing. Isaiah 53: 6 declared that we are ALL sheep that have gone astray...we have all done life our way, and turned our backs to a Holy God. Jesus Christ did not turn His back to us. According to Isaiah 50:6...He gave His back to be beaten...His face to those who pulled the beard from His face. 355 prophecies of the King of Kings coming to earth to save us. Last week, we looked at Stephen in Acts Chapter 7. When he saw Jesus in His Glory, all he could do is forgive them that stoned him. After all that Jesus endured on the cross, He said in Luke 23:34... Father forgive them, for they know not what they do...then the scripture says that they cast lots for His garments, fulfilling the prophecy in Psalm 22. This Word is true!! Jesus proved His love for us. Our repentance is a very good response to recognizing how much He loves us. Forgiving everything completely is another great response. That's what His bruises and stripes and nail scarred hands are all about. We should never be ashamed of the One who died for us (Romans 1:16).

Today...let us must tell the world of this great salvation...Jew or Gentile... Black, White, Asian, Indian...all need to know about the forgiveness, grace, love, and mercy in Jesus Christ... God bless.

$\mathcal{T}$WELVE

24 Now unto him that is able to keep you from falling, and to present you faultless before the presence of his glory with exceeding joy,

Jude 1 :24

He is well able to hold us up. There is so much encouragement in this verse. In 1st Corinthians 10:13...We are told that God will not put more on us than we can bear, and will make a way of escape. We need to take His escape. In Jude 1:24...We are told that Jesus Christ will keep us from falling, and present us faultless. Faultless truly means in right standing with God and forgiven of our sins (we must forgive by the way to get that status...read Mark 11:25-26). In Boy Scout camp in 1974, I took Lifesaving. We were taught as you attempt to rescue a person, they will panic and pull you under too. You see how tough it can be to save someone in a drowning situation. It is just as tough for us to try to save or rescue someone spiritually who wants to fall. But thanks be to God, who gives us the victory through our Lord Jesus Christ. We can pray and say Jesus... please save them. In Hebrews 7:25...He promised to save to the uttermost. He will go to incredible lengths to save, and keep us from falling from His Kingdom. With that much love and mercy poured out on you and I...We should want Him to keep us faultless, and on our way to Glory. Jesus knows how to hold us up, keep us in Him, and get us through.

Today...we should purpose in our hearts to let Jesus hold on tight, clean us up, and get us ready for our eternal home with Him... God bless.

HIRTEEN

13 There hath no temptation taken you but such as is common to man: but God is faithful, who will not suffer you to be tempted above that ye are able; but will with the temptation also make a way to escape, that ye may be able to bear it.

1 Corinthians 10 :13

He knows the breaking point. In Romans 8th chapter, the Word of God tells us that we have been predestined through Jesus to win...to be more than a conqueror. The Word of God in Titus 1:2 says that God cannot lie. In Jude 1:24...we are promised that Jesus is able to keep you from falling...all true and all promises. Yet sometimes we don't "feel" that we are that victorious child of the Most High God. It isn't based on a feeling. When you are feeling overwhelmed and overburdened, and you feel like you want to quit, remember 1st Corinthians 10:13... God will not put more on us than we can take. He knows the breaking point. He knows what snare craftily laid out by satan, will destroy us. So, He promised to make a way of escape. We just need to take the way of escape. When a spirit of bitterness, unforgiveness, or hatred comes at you... escape with love, forgiveness and mercy. That way you remember how much mercy that Jesus gave you and you will not fall. When the circumstances of life seem too heavy or impossible to get through... escape and remember that Jesus loves you. Trust Him, go to your knees, pray, and do what Psalm 27 says... Wait on the Lord...be of good courage. Jesus knows your breaking point. We don't. Our thought on where that is and Jesus' are not going to be the same. Trust the promise of our loving Father... Jesus who knows what to allow and what to stop and when. Remember He promised to keep us from falling. Satan just wants us to feel forsaken, quit, and fall.

Today...say "No" to that lying voice today and every day. You will be more than a conqueror... God bless.

$\mathcal{F}$OURTEEN

10 But He knoweth the way that I take: when He hath tried me, I shall come forth as gold.

Job 23 :10

We go through for our good. We have all been through trials, tribulations and situations that were painful and uncomfortable. We pray and things do not move right away, or in the way that we want or expect. Romans 8:28 and Job 23:10 help give us an answer. Job was in the midst of a terrible trial. God allowed the trial, and actually said to satan "Have you considered my servant Job?" The battle was on...satan accused Job to God... like he does with us (read Revelation 12:10-11). Satan is the accuser of the brethren... that is why we should never take this role one with another. Job's friends spent their time accusing Job, instead of being a friend and praying for him and encouraging him. What we experience is Jesus bringing us through our spiritual childhood and growing us up. Job knew that when God was done with him...he would be pure gold. Romans 8:28 says...and we KNOW that all things work together for good, to them that love God; to them called according to His purpose. Job was blessed with twice as much in the end... double for his trouble (read Isaiah 61: 1-7). Job came through as pure gold and so will we. Jesus promised to never leave you nor forsake you. He did also promise in John 16:33 that in the world we will have tribulations. He also said... Be of good cheer... I have overcome the world. Our tough experiences are bringing us to a knowledge of a God who loves us, put on flesh and went through pain. He knows how to comfort us, grow us and get us through. It all works for our good.

Today... love and trust Jesus. Never do the devil's job and accuse one another. Let's pray one for another...we will all make it through, and like Job... we will be pure gold... God bless

$\mathcal{F}$IFTEEN

10 Be still, and know that I am God: I will be exalted among the heathen, I will be exalted in the earth.

Psalms 46 :10

Jesus is in control. The last several weeks, we have been journeying together. Some of you are going through some of the trials of your life. If you are in a season of peace... Praise God for that season for you. Know assuredly that all seasons change. If you are in a quiet season, pray for those in the battle, dedicate yourself to Jesus, and get built up in the Lord for what may come. For those of us in the battle we have Psalm 46:10...He said... Be still and know that I am God. Be still in your marriage...Be still in your church...stop moving to and fro as Daniel 12 and Ephesians 4 says, and get stable. You and I will never learn Jesus, running around, like a chicken with the spiritual head cut off! Be still and know He is God. We learn to trust Him IN THE STORM. In Mark 4:35-41, the disciples were in a boat with Jesus. A terrible storm came, and the boat was in danger of sinking.

Notice that Jesus was in the boat... but He was asleep. The disciples cried out...Carest thou not that we perish! Don't you care Lord. Jesus stood up and told the storm... Peace be still. Notice He used the words...Be still. The Storm Stopped! Jesus demonstrated that He is God in the flesh, and has all power. If He had the power to stop that storm, He has the power to stop yours and mine. He does not change (Hebrews 13:8). Be still. If a disciple panicked and jumped out of the boat, they would have missed the miracle.

Today, be still and stand still, and allow the King of Kings to calm the storms and bring a glorious victory into your life.

$\mathcal{S}$IXTEEN

22 It is of the LORD's mercies that we are not consumed, because his compassions fail not.

Lamentations 3 :22

Where would we be without His mercy? Why use this same verse again in another devotional message. Perhaps for the same reason that Proverbs 14: 12 and 16: 25 are identical. We need to truly get the message. Mercy is when we do not get we do deserve (Romans 3:23... For all have sinned). Why then is there such a lack of mercy in the church? We seem to forget this verse (we all do) that without HIS mercy we would be consumed. Then there is grace (God's unmerited favor). Grace is us receiving what we don't deserve. Here, the church has taken on the mind of an unrealistic entitlement. Somehow, the mind of God MUST forgive me, and I do not have to forgive others has crept in. I am to get the promises of HIS Word, and have no requirement on me to perform what HIS Word says. John Chapter 1:1-17 tells us that that grace and truth came by Jesus Christ. When Jesus said from the cross..."Father forgive them for they know not what they do... we were given mercy. ** We must give mercy and perform what HIS Word says. His mercy is new every day; please never take this for granted. Romans 6:23 reminds us that the wages of our sins is death. Ecclesiastes 8th Chapter reminds us that judgement against an evil work is NOT executed speedily. Since the mercy is so strong, we tend not to fear or believe Romans 6:23. Jesus came to the rescue with His gift of mercy and forgiveness and salvation. Without His mercy...we would be done...consumed... with no hope. This is why I love Jesus so much. We owed a debt that we could not pay... Jesus paid a debt that He did not owe. I feel the need to repeat this message, but it is the one that unfortunately keeps being missed. We are not consumed and get His new mercy daily. Jesus said in Matthew 7:2 that with the same judgement we measure out, will be measured back to us. I pray that we really believe this!! I frequently quote Mark 11:25-26 for very good reason. Jesus said...if we don't forgive...we are not forgiven. WHY?? Because if I don't measure out the same mercy and forgiveness given to me, I forfeit that mercy. Without the mercy of Jesus Christ, we are doomed to be consumed. Yet according to 1st John 4:19...He loved us first!! Jesus targeted you and I for His love and mercy, even when we weren't thinking about Him.

Today...Show Jesus that we appreciate HIS mercy, by extending love, grace, mercy and true forgiveness to someone else... God bless.

SEVENTEEN

13 He that covereth his sins shall not prosper: but whoso confesseth and forsaketh them shall have mercy.

Proverbs 28 :13

Do you want God's mercy today? This scripture stays right in the theme of 1st Corinthians 10:13... God will not put more on us than we can bear, but gives us a way of escape. Here is the way of escape from guilt and condemnation. Don't hide sin... confess it and forsake the sin. Then you are wide open to be free and delivered. You can receive the mercy of God by saying Lord Jesus... I have done wrong. Do not justify self. Then you have set yourself up for satan beating you over the head with his stick of condemnation. Think about 1st John 1:9...if we confess our sins, He is faithful and just to forgive our sins and cleanse us from all unrighteousness. Jesus will not only forgive us, but will get the messy stuff out of us. If we are honest with Him. 1st John 1:8 says... if we say we have no sin, we are a liar. I am glad that when I stumble, I take the way of escape and repent. I tell Jesus, that I am wrong. I feel a flood of His mercy wash over me. I escaped with repentance, not trying to justify me. He loves us so much, that according to Proverbs 28: 13 we will prosper with forgiveness. That Word of grace came in the Old Testament. In the New Testament...we have a better covenant through the Blood of Jesus. Please do not take the Mercy of God for granted. He says He wants all to come to repentance (2nd Peter 3:9).

Today...please don't justify self today...it's not someone else's fault. It's just all of us, who need to admit our wrongdoing, and receive the Mercy of Jesus... God bless

$\mathscr{E}$IGHTEEN

20 Behold, I stand at the door, and knock: if any man hear my voice, and open the door, I will come in to him, and will sup with him, and He with me.

Revelation 3 :20

I am brought back to this verse again. In Revelation 3:20... Jesus says to the Church at Laodicea... Behold I stand at the door and knock. Revelation Chapters 2 and 3 are actually direct observations of the 7 churches in Asia Minor by Jesus. He spoke to each church, and specifically told them what He saw... good or bad. He praised the Church at Philadelphia for faithfulness, even through the tough times. They would not deny the Name of Jesus...no matter what!! Jesus said...they have an open door and a Heavenly Crown. The Church at Sardis was told that they were not perfect before Him (none of us are by the way). They were told to repent, and to not wait to repent. Jesus did not condemn them for their spiritual shortcomings (Read Romans 8:1...no condemnation in Jesus). He simply said repent... turn away from what does not please God. Laodicea was different. They had wealth and substance.

They believed they had God's favor. Jesus said they were poor, blind and naked. Why is Jesus knocking on the door of their hearts? Why is Jesus outside of His church trying to get in? They crowded Jesus out with pride, self, and a lack of understanding. THEY WERE MISSING THEIR BLESSINGS. They were told to repent too...He didn't condemn them, but did not allow them to be fooled.

Today...let Jesus in!! It's time to kick out pride, bitterness, unforgiveness and the works of the flesh, that keep us in bondage and hinder our blessings. Jesus is knocking today... LET HIM IN... God bless.

$\mathcal{N}$INETEEN

32 And such as do wickedly against the covenant shall He corrupt by flatteries: but the people that do know their God shall be strong, and do exploits.

Daniel 11 :32

What is really going on?? Jesus said in Mark 4:40...Why are ye so fearful? How is it that ye have no faith? Jesus had just calmed a storm in Mark 4:39 with the words " Peace be still". Jesus allowed the terrible storm, and then calmed it, to build the faith of His disciples and let everyone know who He is (God manifested in the flesh...1st Tim 3:16). Why do you have storms going on? Did you need Jesus without the storms? Daniel 11:32 is an end time prophecy. We are in the end times now. THIS IS NOT THE END OF THE WORLD. This is the end of the Church or Gentile age. Jesus made a promise to save Israel...read Zechariah Chapters 10-14. In Romans 11:25, it is called the fullness of the Gentiles. Then the attention of God is on Israel. The troubles in our life are to grow our faith and shake us, so that we know that we need Jesus. In my greatest trial in 1993... I cried out to Jesus. He showed Himself to be awesome in my life. He showed me through the troubles...He can do anything. In these end times... Jesus wants us to do exploits... great things with His power. Time is short, so the storms are many and fierce. We are still more than conquerors through Jesus. The storms are to show that He can still say " Peace be still" to your situation.

Today...surrender... let go of your will and doubt and hard hearted ways today and let Jesus do exploits... you will be more than a conqueror through Him... God bless.

WENTY

33 But seek ye first the kingdom of God, and his righteousness; and all these things shall be added unto you.

Matthew 6 :33

What do we really want... what is life really about? It is truly about Jesus... Not us! We must put Him first. If we say I belong to Jesus, that means that I submit and surrender to His Word and His ways. We say that I pray and God did not do what I want. Well what are you seeking. Is it Jesus first? If so, seek His will first. A man whom I ministered to said ... Well, God said He would give me the desires of my heart. It does say that in Psalm 37... but it said Delight thyself in the Lord...seek Him and put Him first. This is what life is all about. If He is first... You will love the unlovable... forgive the unforgivable... forget the unforgettable. Why?? How?? If the Kingdom of God is first, I am not and never will be on the throne. THAT IS RESERVED FOR JESUS!! I then remember what Jesus said... Let he is without sin cast the first stone. NONE of us is without sin. If we want Jesus to forgive...we must...it is His will !! None of us should put our will over Jesus. For those of us who say we belong to Christ...look at this image...\0/. This is a man with his hands in the air...I know about this with 3 decades in law enforcement... It means I surrender... I give up...the fight is over.

Today...stop fighting Jesus; seek Him first. You will see how glorious life can be with Jesus at the helm of the ship and not you... God bless

$\mathcal{T}$WENTY-ONE

10 The thief cometh not, but for to steal, and to kill, and to destroy: I am come that they might have life, and that they might have it more abundantly.

John 10 :10

A reminder of the what matters...a reminder that this is a very real battle, for your mind and soul. Jesus is God manifested in the flesh (1st Timothy 3:16). He informed His disciples that He is the Good Shepherd. He is the door of salvation (John 1:1-10). Jesus is the hope and Savior of the world. He desires to give us an abundant and victorious life. In Psalm 81:13-14... The Word of God lets us know how much God wants to do in our lives. He wants to do great and mighty things in our lives. He says that we need to follow Him, and actually do what His Word says. Satan is real too, and was defeated when Jesus died on the cross and rose again. The separation between God and man was fixed. In Isaiah 58... Jesus is called The Repairer of the Breach. In the same book of Isaiah, in the 14th chapter...it is clear that one day we will look upon satan and "narrowly consider him". We will be surprised after seeing the Glory and majesty of Jesus, how we could have been so easily deceived by the thief. We will see him as the lying deceiver that he is. Satan lies to us, tries to make us bound by anger, pride, unforgiveness, hatred and bitterness. Jesus said in Matthew 7:9...if a son asks for bread, will you give him a stone? Jesus wants to give salvation, peace, joy, eternal life and victory. He really wants to bless us, but we have got to stop listening to a defeated devil, and FOLLOW victorious Jesus. This is a reminder of who really loves us, and who desires our pain and defeat.

Today...please examine who you follow. We will follow one or the other... Jesus or satan... please follow the one who died for us and repaired the Breach... God bless.

$\mathcal{T}$WENTY-TWO

8 And when He had taken the book, the four beasts and four and twenty elders fell down before the Lamb, having every one of them harps, and golden vials full of odours, which are the prayers of saints.

Revelation 5 :8

A thought about the importance of prayer... This verse in Revelation lines up with Revelation 8: 4. These verses make it clear that our prayers reach Jesus, and they are a sweet savor to Him. He is waiting to hear us, and according to 1st Peter 2:9...we are His Royal Priesthood in the Earth. Jesus wants to hear from us. In Luke 18:1... Jesus said...Men ought always to pray and not to faint. He said in 1st Thessalonians 5:17... The Word of God tells us to Pray without ceasing. Do not quit... continue instant in prayer... Romans 12:12. This is a valuable weapon in our spiritual arsenal...prayer... seeking the face of Jesus... He wants to answer, bring victory, restore families, deliver. heal, change hearts and more. At some of the darkest times in my life... I have felt that someone was truly praying for me. We must pray one for another... Never... Never... with a heart of bitterness and unforgiveness. Why?? You don't want your prayers hindered... you want them to be a sweet savor unto the Lord. You and I want and need miracles to happen. We must pray!! REMEMBER THOUGH... PSALM 66:18... If I regard iniquity in my heart... the Lord will not hear me. I want nothing to hinder one single prayer that I pray to from reaching Jesus... I want Psalm 66:19... verily (truly) thou hast heard me.

Today...let us walk in Psalm 24: 4... with clean hands and a pure heart... forgiving... with love...so that Jesus hears us and brings victory... God bless.

$\mathcal{T}$WENTY-THREE

24 Though He fall, He shall not be utterly cast down: for the LORD upholdeth him with his hand.

Psalms 37 :24

You have a true promise today if you truly hold on to Jesus...HE SAID HE WOULD HOLD ON TO YOU!! Psalm 37 was not written by a young King David, but an old David who had found God to be faithful at every life turn. In verse 23 he wrote...The steps of a good man are ordered by the Lord. In verse 25 David wrote... I have been young, and now am old, yet have I not seen the righteous forsaken, nor his seed begging bread. David knew of God's faithfulness...He trusted Him. David also understood something else... even when he fell short... God was not willing that David should perish, but that he repent, receive God's grace and mercy, and keep pressing in his assignments (2nd Peter 3:9). Satan is the accuser of the brethren (Revelation 12:10). When you and I fail, or fall short,

there is satan to step in and beat us down with guilt and condemnation. He whispers in our ears...see you can't make it...why don't you just quit Jesus and follow me. But look at Psalm 37: 24... Though he fall, he shall not be utterly cast down, for the Lord upholds him with His hand. Jesus died on the cross of Calvary, and said... forgive them, for they know not what they do. What an awesome Saviour!! Simon Peter said...Lord I will never deny you. Jesus said... Peter, you will deny me 3 times. When Peter saw them take Jesus and beat Him and pull out His beard, Peter backed away and denied knowing Jesus. In Matthew 16... Jesus gave Peter the keys to His Kingdom. Then Peter turned on Jesus. Peter ran to the brethren, who demonstrated love and mercy. They did what we should do...Restore!! In John 21... Jesus forgave Peter. Jesus is able to hold us up.

Today, focus on a loving Father, who is well able to pick us up with His loving hands when we fall. God bless.

$\mathcal{T}$WENTY-FOUR

26 Then Moses stood in the gate of the camp, and said, Who is on the LORD's side? let him come unto me. And all the sons of Levi gathered themselves together unto him.

Exodus 32 :26

Know your enemy !! Who is on the Lord's side?? Before any of us are quick to say ME... remember James 1:19 says be slow to speak, swift to hear, and SLOW TO WRATH. If I am on the Lord's side...then I am required to exhibit His character. I am to love like Jesus. I am to forgive like Jesus...then I show that I am on the Lord's side. Remember, Peter denied Jesus...He forgave Peter, never took the keys of the Kingdom from him, and kept him as chief Apostle to the Jews. Manasseh did more wickedly than any other king...once the Lord dealt with him, he repented alone in a cell... God heard him and forgave him, and put him back on the throne. We say we are on the Lord's side, but do we have love, forgiveness and mercy like that. That's why I said be slow to speak...am I really on His side today?? If not, it is probably because of what we read in Exodus 32. Aaron was the brother of Moses. He was the High Priest. Aaron kept listening to the murmuring, complaining and evil communication from Dathan and Korah. Before long the High Priest was making a golden calf and leading Israel into sin. 1st Corinthians 15:33 clearly says... evil communication corrupts good manners...the voice of the enemy brings us out of the favor of a loving, merciful God, to a place where we join the enemy against God's people. Are we really on the Lord's side?? Do we show mercy and love, or do we make Aaron's mistake and incline our ears to God's enemy. Aaron knew the will of God and still got deceived... If we are not careful and prayerful, we could find ourselves on the outs with God and wondering how we got there.

Today...Let us examine ourselves, humble ourselves, and get back to the Lord's side.

TWENTY-FIVE

5 Seek ye the Lord while He may be found, call ye upon Him while He is near:

6 Let the wicked forsake his way, and the unrighteous man his thoughts: and let him return unto the Lord, and He will have mercy upon him: and to our God, for He will abundantly pardon.

Isaiah 55: 6-7

Let's just say that you are sitting on death row...facing a death sentence. Along comes Gov. Hogan and he mercifully grants you a pardon. All is forgiven. Then comes the voice of critics and scoffers. They speak evil of the Governor and his staff... You open your ear and listen to the critics and scoffers... You then surrender your pardon and put yourself back on death row and you give up the free gift of liberty and freedom. Isaiah 55:6-7 says to seek the Lord while He may be found, call upon Him while He is near... He will have mercy...He will grant you His pardon... Rev 21...speaks on the Books of Remembrance... And the Book of Life. Those born again in Jesus... Who say yes to Him... Receive the pardon... Out of the Books... Into the Book. Romans 3:23 says that all have sinned...we all need the pardon. Once you receive the pardon through Jesus... Do not give it away by listening to the critics of Jesus... or the critics of His people...Today let's rejoice in Jesus... Hold on to His nail scarred hand. Remember in 2nd Peter 2nd Chapter God's Word warned us that in the last days, there would be mockers and scoffers who say...Where is the promise of His coming? Jesus has come and lovingly delivered a full pardon to those who will receive it and keep it.

Today, let us focus on the true and awesome mercy of Jesus, and receive and keep His wonderful pardon...God bless

$\mathcal{T}$WENTY-SIX

1 Wherefore seeing we also are compassed about with so great a cloud of witnesses, let us lay aside every weight, and the sin which doth so easily beset us, and let us run with patience the race that is set before us,

Hebrews 12 :1

Time for spiritual weight loss... In Hebrews 12:1, we are told to lay aside every weight and sin that has hindered us and run this race in Jesus with patience (perseverance). You cannot quit and say...It's too hard. You must look to Jesus, the Author and Finisher of our faith (Hebrews 12:2). We also have a great cloud of witnesses who did not quit or make excuses. They used Jesus as the example and got rid of the weight of bitterness, evil thought, unforgiveness, and rebellion. Stephen was stoned for standing for Jesus... He forgave those who stoned him...thus setting up an evil man named Saul of Tarsus to become the Apostle Paul. Paul later forgave John Mark's shortcomings, and said... He is profitable for the ministry (2nd Timothy 4). If you feel weighed down today, it may be because you are holding on to a weight of unforgiveness. Do you want Jesus to hold on to the weight of your sin, and hold it against you??? I think not. Remember if you do not forgive... You are NOT forgiven (Matthew 18:21-35 and Mark 11:25-26). There is no exception to this principle. Why...because our example Jesus said "Father forgive them..." before He hung His head and died on the cross. Consider the Christian woman whose husband was killed by a radical Muslim group. She said... I forgive them...if I don't, how can I win them to Jesus? It's time to look like Jesus, love like Jesus, live like Jesus and forgive like Jesus. We have plenty of witnesses around us who have done just that.

Today, get rid of the weight of every sin and bitterness that would keep us from Glory... God bless

$\mathcal{T}$WENTY-SEVEN

19 Behold, I will do a new thing; now it shall spring forth; shall
ye not know it? I will even make a way in the wilderness, and
rivers in the desert.

Isaiah 43 :19

What powerful Word! Jesus is making sure that we know that He can do anything. Isaiah 43 is an awesome chapter. We have preached many messages from verse 19. He can make a way where there is no way. However, we need to read the whole chapter. In verse 13, God speaks to us and says... I will work and who shall let (stop) it. Who is able to stop the miracle in our life? The answer is... We are !! Jesus can do anything, and wants to show Himself mighty. We stop Him by turning an ear to evil communication and then losing out (1st Cor. 15:33). Or we forget Proverbs 22:24 and connect with the angry and wonder why we have no peace or victory. Winston Churchill said... We have met the enemy and it is us! In Ephesians 3:20, Jesus says He is able to do exceeding abundantly above all that we ask or think, according to the power that worketh in us. The key still comes back to us. Jesus wants to do so much in our lives. Great things! He wants to use us to show His greatness and grow His Awesome Kingdom. He will do that and more if we eliminate negativity, bitterness and unforgiveness.

Today... Let's get out of His way, and see Jesus Christ do His good pleasure in our lives... God bless

$\mathcal{T}$WENTY-EIGHT

37 Nay, in all these things we are more than conquerors through him that loved us.

Romans 8 :37

We are more than conquerors. Again, I am not sending this because all is perfect. I am certain that everyone who receives this today has a battle or situation that you are dealing with. No matter what it is, turn it over to Jesus. When Paul penned this verse, he was in prison for the gospel's sake. He realized that through Jesus...No matter what... He was victorious. The first thing to conquer is self. In Matthew 16:24...Jesus said if any man come after me...he must deny self. You must conquer you through God's Word. Then you are able to say what Job said... Though he slay me, yet will I trust him. He will get you through. You cannot be more than a conqueror, with nothing to conquer. First, conquer you...avoid evil communication, unforgiveness, bitterness and doubt. Then you will see Jesus bring you through whatever the situation. No matter what... Jesus is able. Trust Him... Obey His Word. Get into proper fellowship, so that you know what the will of God is. You can't be a conqueror out of church. Read Hebrews 10:25-26. You were set up to win...to grow through your troubles and give God Glory.

Today, follow the Word of God, forgive, trust and be more than a conqueror through Jesus today... God bless

TWENTY-NINE

4 For thou hast broken the yoke of his burden, and the staff of his shoulder, the rod of his oppressor, as in the day of Midian.

Isaiah 9 :4

He will bring us out !! Today I was blessed with this Word. Just recently Jesus showed me a companion verse to this... Isaiah 10:27...the yoke (burden) is destroyed because of the anointing. Jesus will get us through and bring us out of our trials and tribulations. His anointing (divine presence) will destroy the yoke. I am not making this statement because all is well. In fact, as I am writing this particular message, when everything in my life seems to be in an upheaval. I should be totally discouraged. I should be in total despair. I am writing this because every time I feel the burden becoming too heavy to bear, Jesus sends encouragement. HE keeps me through HIS Word, and HIS divine presence. It is just like Moses holding up his staff, as Joshua waged war on the battlefield. When Moses held up the staff, Israel prevailed. When his arms became too heavy, and the staff came down, Amalek prevailed. Then Aaron and Hur put a rock under Moses, and held his arms up. Then Israel won the battle. That is what Jesus does with HIS encouraging power. HE will bring us out, and HE does hold us up.

Even when enemies come against us...forgive them. By forgiving and praying for your enemies, you unlock all the power of Heaven on your behalf. Jesus has His hand stretched out.

Today, stay in His will, but know... He will bring you and I a great victory... Stay encouraged... God bless

# HIRTY

21 And Elijah came unto all the people, and said, How long halt ye between two opinions? if the LORD be God, follow him: but if Baal, then follow him. And the people answered him not a word.

1 Kings 18 :21

Time to make up your mind. The spiritual warfare and issues of life going on now are intense and fierce. If someone is sitting on the fence, both sides can shoot at them. Make up your mind. Settle in on Jesus today. James 1: 8 says...A double minded man is unstable in all his ways. Romans 4:21 tells us that Abraham was fully persuaded in what God was able to do. He waited 25 years for Isaac to be born. He then tied his son to the altar at God's command. No, there would not be one hair on Isaac's head hurt. God tried Abraham, and he passed his test. Abraham was also fully persuaded that God was able to raise him up. By the way, according to James 5, when Abraham trusted God...He called him His friend. In Matthew 6:24... Jesus said...No man can serve 2 masters. He will love one and despise the other. You can't get a move of God in your life loving Jesus one day and having tea with satan the next day. We want our prayers answered. We cannot say Jesus can on Monday, and Jesus can't on Tuesday. According to Matthew 6:14-15...WE CANNOT SAY JESUS FORGIVE ME, AND THEN NOT FORGIVE SOMEONE ELSE!! Make up your mind. If you have no peace today, it could be that you have not fully surrendered EVERY part of your life to Jesus...The Prince of Peace. When Israel was fully persuaded and sold out to the Lord, no enemy could stand against them. When they flirted with false gods, they lost again and again.

Today...be fully persuaded that Jesus is Lord of your life...stand firm on that, and see His mighty hand move in your life... God bless.

$\mathcal{T}$HIRTY-ONE

1 Truly God is good to Israel, even to such as are of a clean heart.

Psalm 73: 1

4 I cried unto the Lord with my voice, and He heard me out of His holy hill. Se'-lah.

Psalm 4: 4

Psalm 73 is a powerful psalm. The priest looked out and saw the world living without God and apparently prospering. He began to despair inside. He got to the sanctuary of God and the Lord restored his mind and spirit. Psalm 73: 24-26 says...Thou shalt guide me with thy counsel, and afterward receive me to glory. Whom have I in Heaven but thee? And there is none upon earth that I desire beside thee. My heart and my flesh faileth: but God is the strength of my heart, and my portion forever. Sunday, I had some burdens... Some concerns... I felt a bit like the priest in Psalm 73...But Sunday, I went into the sanctuary of Jesus... His Spirit moved into the room. We all began to worship, praise and cry out to Him...I have not been the same since. As the Word of God says... For thou O Lord are a shield for me... my Glory and the lifter up of my head (Psalm 3:3). I have been greatly encouraged by this.

The Steve Green song comes to mind... "People need the Lord" ... At the end of broken dreams, He's our open door. We need Jesus. We need Him so much that words cannot express.

Today, cry out to Jesus. Watch Him lift your burdens, and strengthen your heart...God Bless.

$\mathcal{T}$HIRTY-TWO

Seeing ye have purified your souls in obeying the truth through the Spirit unto unfeigned love of the brethren, see that ye love one another with a pure heart fervently:

1 Peter 1 :22

What is the church grade based on this Word. Does the church in America get an A... In 1st and 2nd Corinthians, the Word of God is clear...LET A MAN EXAMINE HIMSELF !! We are commanded to love with Unfeigned Love. The Word Unfeigned means Genuine. We are to love with genuine pure love. Jesus loves us! He forgave all those who mocked Him and nailed Him to the cross. 39 lashes from a whip, ended up with Jesus saying... Forgive them. The crown of thorns was beaten into the head of God manifested in the flesh... that's who Jesus is...1st Timothy 3:16 says Jesus is God manifested (revealed) in the flesh. He is the Creator, and to save us, He let His creation nail Him to a cross. The result...in Hebrews 8...He promised to remember our sins no more. THAT IS GENUINE UNFEIGNED LOVE. In Acts Chapter 7... Stephen prayed for those who stoned him to death. He said... Lord lay not this sin to their charge...He forgave all... everything. In John 13... Jesus said that men would know that we are His disciples (not just believers, but disciples) by our love one for another. Look in the mirror of these scriptures. Grade yourself based on the standard of the Word of God. Am I a disciple? Do I truly love and forgive? Do I hold a grudge? Do I remember the sins of my brother or sister? DO YOU WANT JESUS TO REMEMBER YOURS? Please grade yourself based on the Word...not opinion. Do I truly love? Our eternal destiny may very be determined by our answer.

Today...Let's love like Jesus loves us... God bless.

$\mathcal{T}$HIRTY-THREE

7 So that contrariwise ye ought rather to forgive him, and comfort him, lest perhaps such a one should be swallowed up with overmuch sorrow.

2 Corinthians 2 :7

Our day to need this mercy will come...in 1st Corinthians 5...the Apostle Paul addressed the issue of a man who had sinned. Here in 2nd Corinthians, we see God's Word saying to us... FORGIVE him. Please read 2nd Corinthians 2:6-11 today, and let us not be ignorant of satan's devices. The devil is the enemy of our souls. He is called in 1st John 4th Chapter...the father of lies. He wants us to condemn ourselves, and CONDEMN OTHERS. Any time that there is vengeance in the heart...IT IS NOT GOD !! Anytime there is unforgiveness, It Is Not God!! Paul said that the man should be forgiven. That is the mercy that we should want and need. Matthew 7 is clear...the same level of mercy we give is the same that we will receive. Our day of needing mercy is... every day. Let us remember how soon the return of Jesus is and forgive and have clean hands and a pure heart. Paul wrote and told the Church at Corinth, and even though the man had done wrong, he should be forgiven. In today's climate of bitterness, Paul's admonition seems to fall on deaf ears, in and out of the church. Our environment today says to hold everyone's offenses against them. Jesus said in Mark 11: 25-26, if we do not forgive, we are not forgiven.

Today, let's remember how much we have been forgiven for, and truly forgive and restore others...God bless

$\mathcal{T}$HIRTY-FOUR

15 For He saith to Moses, I will have mercy on whom I will have mercy, and I will have compassion on whom I will have compassion.

Romans 9 :15

In Romans 9:15...the scripture reminds us that God is merciful. Psalm 136 says that His mercy endureth forever. He will pour out His love, mercy and compassion where and when He chooses. We have all gotten mercy and felt Jesus' compassion in our time of need.

Jesus is the perfect judge of where mercy is needed and how much is needed. Since Romans 3:23 says...For all have sinned and come short of the glory of God... WE ALL NEED MERCY. Jesus said in Matthew 6...if you don't forgive...you won't be forgiven. If we don't give mercy, how then do we expect mercy from the Lord. I want Jesus to give me mercy and grace. He said in Matthew 5:7...blessed are the merciful, for they shall obtain mercy. I am certain of my need to give mercy, because I have received so much mercy. The thing we do not realize about New Testament grace is that it deals with our heart toward one another. That is a higher standard than the law, that showed us what is wrong with our actions. Grace requires us to be forgiving and merciful at a heart level.

Today, be merciful and forgiving, and receive the Grace and Mercy of God... God bless

$\mathcal{T}$HIRTY-FIVE

58 Therefore, my beloved brethren, be ye stedfast, unmoveable,
always abounding in the work of the Lord, forasmuch as ye know
that your labour is not in vain in the Lord.

1 Corinthians 15 :58

With all the storms of life and trials, we must do as David did in 1st Samuel 30 and encourage ourselves in the Lord. The how is in 1st Corinthians 15:58...Be steadfast and unmovable, and know that your labor is not in vain in the Lord. Do not waiver in the midst of the storm; Jesus is looking for opportunity to show you and I off, as a literal lighthouse, standing in the darkness.

Jesus remembers our labor of love, our steadfastness and faithfulness. He sees when we are going through, and sends help. He helped David in his time of trouble, and He will help us. David was in an incredible time of trouble. His family had been taken, and his camp burned. His own men thought of stoning him. He did not turn on God, he turned to God, and encouraged himself in the Lord. He was steadfast and unmoveable. We have a better covenant than David had with the Lord. He is reminding us to persevere, press on...don't quit, and avoid evil communication. The result will be 1st Corinthians 15:57...Now thanks be unto God, which always gives us the victory through our Lord Jesus Christ.

Today, be steadfast and unmoveable, and encourage yourself in the Lord Jesus Christ... God bless.

$\mathscr{T}$HIRTY-SIX

14 Because strait is the gate, and narrow is the way, which leadeth unto life, and few there be that find it.

Matthew 7 :14

Jesus told us in Matthew 7:13-14 to enter in at the straight gate. He said that the broad way leads to destruction. He made it clear that the narrow way leads to life; And Few There Be That Find It! Most take the broad way because it's quite easy to the flesh. The broad way says I only have to believe. I don't have to change... I don't have to die to my will and live for Jesus' will. The broad way omits the scriptural fact that you must be born again (John 3:1-7)...You must forgive. The broad way says...Well, I forgive, but I don't forget. There is racism in the broad way, hatred gossip and bitterness. ** Then there is the narrow way... This leads to life. There is true Agape love in the narrow way. You forgive in the narrow way and release all offenses. The narrow way does not point fingers or speak evil.

** The narrow way remembers my own sin and understands forgiveness, mercy and redemption... There is no gossiping, backbiting, racism, unforgiveness, hatred or discord. The narrow way leads to life...Jesus said FEW find it...

Today take the narrow way, and have victory in the Word of God... God bless

$\mathcal{T}$HIRTY-SEVEN

13-14

Let us hear the conclusion of the whole matter; fear God and keep
His commandments, for this is the whole duty of man. For God,
shall bring every work into judgement, with every secret thing,
whether it be good or whether it be evil

Ecclesiastes 12:13-14

The meaning of life... Wise or foolish...Ecclesiastes 12: 13-14 Let us hear the conclusion of the whole matter; fear God and keep His commandments, for this is the whole duty of man. For God, shall bring every work into judgement, with every secret thing, whether it be good or whether it be evil. Jesus, in Matthew 25: 1-13 spoke of the wise and the foolish... Those who keep the fear (reverence) of God in their heart are wise...those who keep in close relationship to Jesus, with oil in their lamp...keeping the Word of God... Loving and forgiving one another... That is wisdom. The two wisest ever spoke again and again about wisdom. Solomon in Ecclesiastes and Jesus in Matthew 25 and Matthew 10:28 agreed that the fear of God leads to success in life. You will be ready when Jesus returns...oil in your lamp, souls won for Jesus... No hatred or bitterness in heart. Here we see what life is all about. Not missing opportunities to impact the lives of others for Jesus. Not missing the opportunity to forgive someone and set them free.

Today, walk in wisdom; walk obediently with Jesus... Walking in victory and a fulfilling life in Jesus Christ...God bless

$\mathcal{T}$HIRTY-EIGHT

2 Set your affection on things above, not on things on the earth.

Colossians 3 :2

Jesus said in the sermon on the mount... Where your treasure is, there will your heart be also (Matthew 6:21). He said, Lay up your treasure in Heaven, where moth and rust doth not corrupt. If I set my affection on Jesus, I become a partaker in His holiness, His righteousness, His covenant promises. Where is your affection today? Jesus watched over you while you slept. He kept you protected and safe. The deer didn't run across your path when you were driving. You spun out, and regained control of the car. The armed robber chose somebody else. I think you get the message. How about this...your spouse said that they were never coming home, and they did. Your runaway child is now back at home. Those are all great things that Jesus did. How about just blessing HIS Kingdom, just for who HE is? Let us set our affection on Jesus Christ the Author and Finisher of our faith. Remember, what we do for Him has eternal benefit and reward. Hebrews 6:10 says...God is not unjust to forget your work and labour of love, which ye have showed toward His name, in that ye have ministered to the saints and do minister. He has a Book of Life. He remembers our good works. He has an eternal reward for us. Jesus said in John 14...I go to prepare a place for you. We love Him, because He first loved us (1st John 4: 19).

Today, tell someone of His goodness ...Jesus...King of Kings and Lord of Lords... God bless.

$\mathcal{T}$HIRTY-NINE

24 For I tell you, that many prophets and kings have desired to see those things which ye see, and have not seen them; and to hear those things which ye hear, and have not heard them.

Luke 10:24

22-23 And it shall come to pass, while My glory passeth by, that I will put thee in the cleft of the rock, and will cover thee with my hand while I pass by. 23 And I will take away mine hand, and thou shalt see my back parts, but my face shall not be seen.

EXODUS 33:22-23

We are so blessed to have Jesus and His Word and His Spirit in the fullness. Moses was a great and mighty man of God. He was the deliverer, mightily used to bring the Children of Israel out of captivity in Egypt. Moses saw the burning bush. Moses penned the first five books of the Bible. Moses was used to bring the Children of Israel out of Egyptian bondage. He raised his staff, and saw the Red sea part. He struck a rock, and water came out. The thing to meditate on today, is that with all of the miracles that Moses was used to perform, he just wanted to see the Glory of God in a more intimate way. He wanted a closer relationship with the God of Abraham, Isaac, and Jacob. He asked to see God's Glory. What a heart!! The miracles were not enough for Moses. When he wanted to see the Glory of God, Moses was told that God would pass by him, and hide him in the cleft of the rock. He would only allow Moses to see the 'Hinder Parts", not the Face of God. David was the same as Moses, and in Psalm after Psalm, he longed for a more intimate and person relationship. In Isaiah Chapter 38, Hezekiah was miraculously healed by the Lord. He said in verse 19…The living, the living shall praise thee as I do this day. He rejoiced in God's miracle, but like David desired to be closer to God.

In Luke 10;24, Jesus told His disciples that many prophets and kings desired to see what His disciples saw and experienced. 2nd Corinthians 4: 6 says that the Glory of God shines in our hearts, revealed in the face of Jesus Christ. We get the fullness!! We can have an intimacy with Jesus that the Old Testament saints longed for. We can have the Glory of God on the inside, because of the Cross of Calvary. The book of Hebrews says 14 times that we have a better, more excellent covenant. We do not just see the "Hinder Parts", we have Jesus in a face to face, more intimate way.

Today, please meditate on how awesome our New Testament relationship with Jesus Christ really is. We have a relationship closer than that of Moses or even David. Keep that thought in your heart and mind today… God Bless.

$\mathcal{F}$ORTY

1 And He spake a parable to this end, that men ought always to pray and not to faint.

Luke 18: 1

Luke 18:1 says men ought always to pray and not faint. Jesus spoke in parable about a woman who pleaded her case to an unjust judge. He was a man who did not fear God or man. The woman continually petitioned the judge, again and again. Her cause was so important to her that she would not stop pleading her cause to the unjust judge. Eventually, the unjust judge became weary of the continual pleading. He said that even though he did not regard God or man, he would fix her problem and move on her behalf. How many times are we in a situation so painful that you continually pray about it. You even add days of fasting and intense prayer day and night. I have been there several times in my life. These are not enjoyable times. You and I need things to miraculously move. I have had a situation so tough, that I truly felt like Job. The weapon that we have against impossible situations, is praying to Jesus, the God of the possible. 1st Thessalonians 5: 17 says "PRAY WITHOUT CEASING". In other words, pray and don't quit. This is one of the most heartfelt messages that I can share with you. We pray sometimes, and it gets worse. I know this is the case. The woman in Luke 18, just kept pleading her case to the judge. I am writing this devotional in one of those seasons where you can't help feeling like the burden is too great, and quitting seems like the thing to do. I know that I am speaking to someone, who is in the fiercest battle of their life. I can tell you since this is a ship that no one wants to sail on, however it is inevitable. No matter what you are going through, pray and don't quit. You may feel alone and abandoned. Pray, and don't quit. It may be severe trouble with you husband, wife, or children. Pray and don't quit. It may be a major financial crisis. Pray, and don't quit. It may be extremely tough, but Jesus will answer, and that right early.

Today, do not quit on Jesus...Keep praying and believing... God bless

$\mathcal{F}$ORTY-ONE

27 Peace I leave with you, my peace I give unto you: not as the world giveth, give I unto you. Let not your heart be troubled, neither let it be afraid.

John 14 :27

Jesus cannot lie. He promised to give us peace. We must receive the peace that He promised. His peace is not like the world's peace. Jesus' peace is like the eye of a hurricane. When everything is seemingly spinning out of control, we have His promise of comfort. In 2nd Corinthians 1, Jesus is revealed to us as the God of Comfort (verses 3-7). The Eye of the hurricane is a good way to look at what storm you are in right now. Everything appears to be a terrible blowing wind. There is a place of peace and victory in the midst of the storm. It is the Eye of life's hurricanes. Jesus said, Peace I leave with you". He also said in that fourteenth chapter of John, "I will not leave you comfortless, I WILL COME TO YOU"(verse 18). Jesus also said...Let not your heart be troubled, neither let it be afraid. 1st John 4:18 says that fear carries torment. In the midst of the troubles, Jesus is the only one who can give us a peace that passes all understanding (Philippians 4:7). Just look at the current news events. There is no peace in the world. There is fear, hatred, bitterness, and unforgiveness in the world. In Jesus, there is an amazing peace, that can penetrate the worst situations, and strengthen, stablish, and settle you (1st Peter 5:10).

Today...Let's receive His Word and His peace today That is one of His true, awesome promises...God bless.

$\mathcal{F}$ORTY-TWO

*1 I will bless the LORD at all times: his praise shall continually
be in my mouth.*

Psalms 34 :1

A great Word and a great way to maintain victory. King David wrote in
Psalm 34: 1…I will bless the Lord at all times; His praise shall continually
be in my mouth. When David wrote this Psalm, he was in very tough place.
He was hiding in a cave. He was not only running away from King Saul, his
father in law, but he also had to flee from King Abimelech of the Philistines.
He was alienated from his wife and family. He was alienated from his people.
David was in a very tough place. I have been in the place of aloneness and
alienation. I felt like David, and even had the Elijah emotion that it's me
and just me left. I am speaking to someone, who is experiencing a spouse
leaving or children rebelling, and even running away. You may be facing a
seemingly insurmountable financial matter. May I tell you today that every
human emotion is going to run through your head. You may want to quit,
give up and say what satan wants you to say…FORGET IT!!

Please take the David route instead. I will bless the Lord at all times. All
truly means all. Give Jesus praise, tell HIM that HE is first in your life, and
praise HIM. No, our intellect says be frustrated. I have been there too. I have
received some of the greatest victories in my life through praise, and turning
my heart to love Jesus, the God of my salvation. He must love me, because
HE died for me. Since Jesus loves me, and proved it, why don't we just praise
HIM through the hard times!

Today, no matter how things look, no matter how you feel, bless the Lord
and give Him Glory…God Bless.

$\mathcal{F}$ORTY-THREE

*20 Now unto Him who is able to do exceeding abundantly above
all that we ask of think, according to the power that worketh in us.*

Ephesians 3: 20

*3 Call unto me and I will answer thee, and show thee great and
mighty things thou knowest not.*

Jeremiah 33: 3

Ephesians 3:20 says ... Now unto Him, who us able to do exceeding abundantly above all that we ask or think, according to the power that worketh in us... Jeremiah 33 3 says ...Call unto Me and I will answer thee and show thee great and mighty things thou knowest not. Jesus can do and help...way more than we think... We need to ask... And we need to believe... Get away from doubt and negativity... Then watch Jesus move on your behalf. HE is not limited. We limit HIM. Psalm 78: 41 reminds us that Israel limited the HOLY ONE of Israel. Jesus is ready and waiting to help us. I know this to be true through very bad circumstances. At the very tough and dark times, Jesus wants to show Himself mighty. HE truly wants a lost world to know just how awesome HE and how much HE can truly help you. The thing that Jesus does may very well be to correct and purify your heart first. I have seen Him do great things, but remember the part of Ephesians 3: 20 that says, according to the power that worketh in us. The work in us may need to happen before HE sends the miracle. Jesus can do anything that we think, and even greater. He may need you to forgive, or get the bitterness out of you, BEFORE HE sends the great and mighty thing. I had a powerful move of HIS Spirit one night, and Jesus that brought me closer to HIMSELF, and essentially was my Garden of Gethsemane. It was a place of self-death to my will. The "Exceeding Abundantly" came after that night. Jesus literally removed the bitterness of a matter out of me. He began to do great things right away.

Today...Believe Jesus for great and mighty things; but check your heart condition to bring them to pass.

$\mathcal{F}$ORTY-FOUR

1 Not unto us, O LORD, not unto us, but unto thy name give glory, for thy mercy, and for thy truth's sake.

Psalms 115 :1

All glory and honor and praise belongs to Jesus, and His marvelous all powerful name !! My time recovering from hip surgery has done something incredible in my life. I have had a lot of time with Jesus...in prayer, Word and worship. I have seen that life is not about us. It is about Jesus !! The psalmist wrote... Not to us O Lord... but to thy Name give Glory. Verse 2 in Psalm makes it clear that no one should ever say...Where is your God? Verse 3 says that God is in the heavens, and He has done whatsoever He pleased. Jesus is worthy of the Praise!! He is awesome. He has sustained so many through hurricanes, floods, fires and troubles. He has proven Himself to be so incredibly real through things that I have faced recently, and so many of you have had the same experience. People around us see our troubles and pain and see us endure. When it looks like we should just throw in the towel...we stand up and tell someone about the goodness of Jesus. Not to us O Lord...but to you our loving Father get the Praise!! In my alone time, in physical and emotional pain, I began to just Praise Jesus for His loving kindness and tender mercy. Note that the pain of my recovery is REALLY there. The pain of some life events is REALLY there. When my attention moved off of me and on to Jesus, I felt His love and comfort... bitterness left me!! I felt hidden unforgiveness leave me (we ALL have them inside...we ALL need Jesus to show us where it is). I then began to preach Jesus to a staff member here, who began to repent, cry and say... I need Jesus!! The person I spoke to knew about some of my trials. I just told them about the God of salvation, who can get you through.

Today... Love and Praise God and see His Glory... God bless

$\mathcal{F}$ORTY-FIVE

10-13

10 And ye shall hallow the fiftieth year, and proclaim liberty throughout all the land unto all the inhabitants thereof: it shall be a jubilee unto you; and ye shall return every man unto his possession, and ye shall return every man unto his family.

11 A jubilee shall that fiftieth year be unto you: ye shall not sow, neither reap that which groweth of itself in it, nor gather the grapes in it of thy vine undressed.

Leviticus 25: 10-13

A thought for EVERY new year:

In Leviticus 25th chapter, the children of Israel were given an event called Jubilee... It was the Lord's release... a forgiveness of all debts and burden...all were made free at this time. In a time that a new year comes, every mistake of the previous year is history. It is in the past. The Word of God made provision and created a system to forget and forgive debts of the past. Remember the Word of God in Philippians 3...Paul wrote...forgetting those things that are behind me... I press toward the mark of the High calling of God in Christ Jesus. Hebrews 6: 18 states that is impossible for God to lie. In Hebrews 8th Chapter, Paul also writes in verses 10 to 12, I will remember their sins and iniquities no more. God set up a system of releasing you from the past. If you have been bitten by the bug of failure (we all have) get up and don't stay down. If you have been hurt or offended (we all have) release it!! Let's take a Jubilee and let go of the defeats of the past year. If you had a victory... Give the glory to Jesus... If you had a failure, put it behind you. Grab the nail scarred hand of Jesus and walk in victory.

Today, when a new year comes, even a new season, or even a new day (Lamentations 3 confirms this) forgive and release all offenses. Forgive others, and by all means...FORGIVE YOURSELF...God bless.

ℐORTY-SIX

21 This I recall to my mind therefore have I hope.

22 It is of the Lord's mercies that we are not consumed, because His compassions fail not.

23 They are new every morning, great is thy faithfulness.

24 The Lord is my portion saith my soul, therefore will I hope in Him.

Lamentations 3: 21-24

Jesus is so very faithful. We should be and think like Him. He is so merciful and forgiving, that at the dawning of a new day, He extends new mercy to His children. He is so forgiving that He is faithful not to hold yesterday against us. Remember that Titus 1: 2 says that…God Cannot Lie. If He says that His mercy is new every morning…IT IS !! In John Chapter 8, Jesus looked at woman "caught" in adultery, and judged her actions, and the actions of the crowd that brought her to Him. They quoted the Law of Moses (incorrectly) and said that she should be stone. Actually, the man and the woman were to receive the same judgement, but the crowd was attempting to trick Jesus. (Can you imagine being so blind that you believe that you can fool God manifested in the flesh?)…Jesus ignored their words and just wrote in the dirt. He then said, "Let he who is WITHOUT sin cast the first stone at her". They dropped their stones, and walked away. Jesus asked the woman… Where are your accusers? She said that there were none. Jesus said, Neither, do I condemn you. Go, and sin no more".

What a loving, faithful and forgiving Saviour. Why then do WE condemn one another, and refuse to forgive one another? Why do WE hold one another's offenses against each other? Jesus promises to forgive us when we ask, and in mercy that faithful to do so. ** He makes one clear stipulation though...Per Mark 11: 25-26, Matthew 6: 14-15, and Matthew 18: 21-35, if we do not forgive...WE ARE NOT FORGIVEN. Since Jesus is so faithful to forgive us, we MUST faithfully and unconditionally forgive. ** We cannot say that the offending party did not come repenting to me, so I do not have to forgive. I am sorry, but that FALSE theological thought is directly opposed to the loving, merciful way that Jesus forgives us. We have so many things that we have done, that we don't even know are sin. You know, the "acceptable" church sins. How many have had a heart of pride, racism, lust, a little coveting, or gossip. Since we all stand guilty, we need Jesus to forgive us. We then must remember the forgiveness and mercy of our God.

Today, remember the new mercies of Jesus. Forgive with the same loving passion that he forgives us...UNCONDITIONALLY !!

ℱORTY-SEVEN

4 Ye adulterers and adulteresses, know ye not that the friendship of the world is enmity with God? whosoever therefore will be a friend of the world is the enemy of God.

James 4 :4

15 Love not the world, neither the things that are in the world. If any man love the world, the love of the Father is not in him.

1ˢᵗ John 2:15

PLEASE DO NOT TAKE THIS THE WRONG WAY !! In Galatians 4: 16, Paul writes…Am I therefore your enemy, because I tell you the truth? Please do not get offended at the words adulterers and adulteresses.

In Psalm 4:3…Jesus makes it clear… Know that the Lord has set him that is Godly apart for Himself. Jesus loves you and I so much, that HE does not want to share you with the world. He hears our prayers, and made very clear promises to answer those prayers. If you were in a stadium with 80,000 others, and you cried out to Jesus; HE would hear you. If we have relationship with Him…you have HIS ear. He does not want to share us with a rebellious world. Remember today that we have been called out of the world. We are to be a different people, with different desires. We are to evangelize and bring the lost out…not attach ourselves to the lost. Jesus is a jealous God, and rightfully so. He died on the cross to give us eternal life, and the forgiveness of sins. HE poured HIS Spirit out to us, and actually dwells on the inside of us. We have a better relationship that the Old Testament saints, who could only have God anoint them on the outside. Now you see why he does not want you to commit spiritual adultery, by giving yourself to other gods of the world.

Today… Remember that Jesus has set you apart, not to be like everyone else, but to show them the true value of a separated life unto HIM…God bless

FORTY-EIGHT

15 Whoso hateth his brother is a murderer: and ye know that no murderer has eternal life abiding in him.

1ˢᵗ John 3: 15

20 If a man say I love God and hateth his brother, he is a liar: for he that loveth not his brother whom he hath seen, how can he love God whom he hath not seen?

Tell me if this is something that you have said from time to time. Well, at least I have not killed anybody. sometimes we justify the stuff down on the inside of us. In Ecclesiastes 12:14 a powerful thought was written by Solomon. Verse 14 states...For God shall bring whether it be evil. There is no way to hide God's truth; he knows everything about us. The standard of how much we love one another is so much greater in the age of grace, than under the law. The law showed me where my actions are wrong. In grace (new testament unmerited favor of God) our heart, thoughts and motives are on trial. We have to have what Psalm 24: 4...Clean hands and a pure heart. If I hate my brother or sister, I have become a murderer and a liar. That is not my opinion. It is directly stated in the above verses. I often think of how important it is to love and forgive no matter what. I PLAN TO MAKE IT TO HEAVEN TO BE WITH JESUS FOREVER !! Since that is my full and unwavering intention (I hope it is yours too), I forgive everybody, everything, and switch thoughts of hatred to love. Rejection must be replaced with a mind of prayer and intercession. I am not a murderer or a liar. I must keep that thought no matter what. You know that you have been tried on this, and since satan is the enemy of our souls, he will continually try to make us get and stay angry at one another. He then will try to get you and I to hide the anger, and miss our blessings and the Glory of Heaven.

Today, fall in love with Jesus, and let us truly love one another. Show that the devil is a liar when he tries to say that you are a murderer or a liar...God Bless.

51

*F*ORTY-NINE

8 Our help is in the name of the LORD, who made heaven and earth.

Psalms 124 :8

1 God is our refuge and strength, a very present help in trouble.

Psalm 46:1

Our only true help is the Name of Jesus. Psalm 46: 1 says He is a very present help in trouble. Some of you are in a troubled situation. You feel like Daniel in the Lion's Den. You feel like the 3 Hebrew boys in the firey furnace. I have been there too. Sometimes you feel alone, like the Apostle John on the Isle of Patmos. You are in a situation that is uncomfortable, and truly impossible for man to solve. Jesus is often the author of you and I being in that situation. He wants us to trust HIM. HE wants to show Himself mighty. He is a very present help in trouble. Sometimes the trouble is part of the very present help. When you get to Heaven, ask Lazarus. Amazingly, Jesus waited until he was 4 days dead to show up at the tomb and raised him up. You see that same I am still on time character when God raised the son of the widow at Zarapath, and the son of the Shunamite woman from the dead. He knows how tough your situation is, and is a very present help. The Name of the Lord is a strong tower; the righteous runneth into it and is safe. The Name of Jesus is a very mighty, and very present help in trouble.

Today...Let us call on the Name of the King of kings and Lord of Lords...our true help and true God...Jesus

$\mathcal{F}$IFTY

1 Truly God is good to Israel, even to such as are of a clean heart.

2 But as for me, my feet were almost gone: my steps had well nigh slipped.

3 For I was envious of the foolish, when I saw the prosperity of the wicked.

Psalm 73: 1-3

9 All this have I seen, and applied to my heart unto every work that is done under the sun: there is time wherein one man ruleth over another to his own hurt.

Ecclesiastes 8:9

We have all been here. The priest was looking out of his window, and saw the ungodly having a good time. He began to envy the wicked. We have had this emotion sometimes, when those we love or care about, or even just work with appear to be living prosperously, in a manner contrary to the Word of God. They appear that they are winning. Sometimes they may even throw a few choice comments to you. You feel like an old shoe, or a punching bag. It is amazing how satan moves people to attack verbally and hurt. The world sometimes just seems to be on top. So, the priest is Psalm 73 began to envy the foolish and wicked. For a moment, he did not see the incredible value that his relationship with God meant, or the eternal reward.

In the 17th verse of Psalm 73, the priest received a Word in due season to help him understand. He said, "Until I went into the sanctuary of God; then understood I their end". He received the encouragement in righteousness that he needed to keep pressing with the Lord. Suddenly he knew that the unrighteous are winning today, but one day all of us will stand before the judgement seat of Christ (2nd Corinthians 5:10). One day, it will not be well with the wicked. They rule to their own hurt. The place of victory over righteous living is temporary.

Today...let us all get to the Sanctuary of God, and know that there is great value in living for Jesus. Stay encouraged in righteousness, and do not be deceived by the fleeting and temporary prosperity of wickedness...God Bless.

$\mathcal{F}$IFTY-ONE

20 Thou leddest thy people like a flock by the hand of Moses and Aaron.

Psalm 77: 20

11 I am the Good Shepherd: The Good Shepherd giveth His life for the sheep.

John 10:11

In Psalm 77:20...the Word says that God led His people as a flock, by the hand of Moses and Aaron...In John 10...Jesus says He is the Good Shepherd, who gives his life for the sheep. A sheep is a very interesting creature to use as an example for the children of God. A sheep is a defenseless animal, that is very, very dependent on the Shepherd. The Shepherd leads the sheep go good, still waters (you see sheep will no drink from running waters). Remember David's words in Psalm 23...The Lord is my shepherd; I shall not want. He makes me to lie down in green pastures; He leads me beside still waters; He restores my soul. I am very glad to have the heart and mind of the sheep today. It was not always so with me. Maybe you have the same testimony. Maybe you were very proud, and the idea of being a sheep was far off from your thinking. I was a Drug-Free National Powerlifting Champion in 1989, 1991, and 1992. I set the American Record in the Squat at 944 pounds in 1993. I always found it amazing that Jesus brought me to salvation in HIM in 1993. I was at my proudest point of my life. I was surely NOT a sheep. I was more like a hard-headed goat.

It is also amazing to me that Jesus laid out the difference between those who will follow HIM, and those who won't in Matthew 25: 32-33. Jesus said that HE will divide the world as a shepherd divides sheep from goats. Jesus likened the rebellious who will not hear HIS Word to goats. Those who will follow HIM, and depend on the Shepherd, he called sheep. In Psalm 77, we see that God led HIS people through the wilderness as sheep. HE used Moses and Aaron to carry out HIS will. Jesus wants to lead us, and HE really is the "Good Shepherd".

Today…you have a choice …be a sheep being led to victory, or a goat following his own way to destruction… Be a sheep today… God bless

$\mathcal{F}$IFTY-TWO

1 Therefore seeing we have this ministry, as we have received mercy, we faint not;

2 Corinthians 4:1

Though the outward man perish, yet the inward man is renewed day by day.

2nd Corinthians 4:16

We have received an awesome gift in Christ Jesus. We have been given a ministry of power, authority, and reconciliation. Jesus has chosen us to receive the truth of His Word, the power of His resurrection and the fellowship of His suffering. Given all that Jesus has empowered us with, as the warfare of these end times intensifies, we do not quit during the fight. Basically, when it gets tough (and it will)... Don't faint, and don't quit.

If I were writing this to you with no storms raging, then you could say; "Easy for bring you to say!". If only you were going through what I am going through, then you would understand. I can assure you that I am writing this message to you when one of the fiercest (if not the fiercest) storm has ever gone on in my life. I cannot quit on Jesus, and either can you! Someone who needs Jesus is watching. Someone who is going through a traumatic time needs to know that suicide is NOT the answer. They need to know that Psalm 46:1 is true...God is our refuge and strength; a very PRESENT help in trouble. Jesus is sustaining me through this trial; HE will sustain you. HE is not a respecter of persons (James 2:1-13...Romans 2:11). Please trust Jesus; the Lord of Glory to get you through. Do not quit on the only one who can bring the victory in your situation. Whether your crisis is spiritual, familial, financial, marital, or health...Jesus is your only answer and solution. I know this to be the case. Like Abraham, I am fully persuaded that Jesus Christ is well able to bring you through, and even bring you out of any situation or trial.

Today...remember that Jesus Christ has all power, and wants to bring you out of you troubles. Even if the trouble persists, HE is able to keep you through them. God Bless.

FIFTY-THREE

8 Oh that men would praise the LORD for his goodness, and for his wonderful works to the children of men!

Psalms 107 :8

Two things to meditate on when we think about how awesome Jesus is. In Psalm 107, the Psalmist wrote a history of how God led the Children of Israel through the wilderness. Verse 6 reads...then they cried unto the Lord in their trouble, and HE delivered them out of their distresses. Verse 8, 15, 21 and 31 all read the same. Oh, that men would praise the Lord for HIS goodness, and HIS wonderful works to the children of men. Jesus wants us to acknowledge how good HIS wonderful works are. We should praise HIM for the battles HE fights and the victories that HE brings. HE wants us to remember that Jesus is our Good Shepherd and an awesome provider. BUT...It is also so very important to praise Jesus and give HIM Glory for WHO HE IS!! Note that these 4 verses remind us that HE does great things, but it is so very important to just think on how awesome and loving Jesus is. A Holy God, who knows no sin, put on flesh to save us from our sin. He took the punishment for everything I have done wrong, do wrong, and will do wrong. That's why we should just praise HIM for who HE is. A Just God and a Saviour. He is King of Kings and Lord of Lords. He is worthy of praise, and the very thought of that brings me to loving what is unlovable. His glory makes me Forgive the unforgivable... ALL THE TIME FOR EVERYTHING. I am pressed in my spirit to tell the world about Jesus. Oh, that men would praise the Lord for HIS goodness, and HIS wonderful works to the children of men.

Today... let's not wait until the time of trouble. Let's praise Jesus, love like HIM, forgive like HIM; just because of who HE is. God bless.

ℱIFTY-FOUR

23-24 But the hour cometh, and now is, when the true worshippers shall worship the Father is spirit and in truth: for the Father seeketh such to worship him.

God is a Spirit: and they that worship HIM must worship HIM in spirit and in truth.

John 4: 23-24

There is a way that Jesus wants us to worship HIM. If you see Old Testament references to worship, it is clear that there was a separation between God and man. When men and women sought a Word from the Lord, they came to a priest to intercede for them. They came to the prophets for understanding, revelation, and instruction. If you had a sin that the LAW of Moses made you aware of, you had to bring a lamb, ram, bull, or turtledove to offer to have your sin covered. You could only have the Spirit of the Lord on the outside. God did not indwell man, because of a separation called "sin". There was a veil in the Temple, which separated the Inner Court from the Holy of Holies, or "Most Holy Place". Then Jesus died on the Cross of Calvary. The thick veil was torn from top to bottom upon HIS death, indicating that the Hand of God Himself tore the veil.

Now true worship can take place. Now we can approach The Father, and know that our prayers are heard, and that a Holy God will bend HIS ear to hear us. The very Spirit of God came to dwell in man in the 2nd Chapter of the Book of Acts. Now man had true relationship with God, in the Name of Jesus!! We can worship in spirit and truth; we can call on HIS wonderful name. We have instant access to Heaven, and complete forgiveness of sin, when we ask. We now have the promise of 1st John 1:9...If we confess our sins, He is faithful and just to forgive us our sins, and cleanse us from all unrighteousness. We have 66 books of how to walk with Jesus, and love one another.

Today...Let's seek the Face of God, and truly come to HIM is a submitted, humble, and open way of spirit and truth. Let's all decrease, and worship Jesus, so that HE can truly increase in us. God Bless.

$\mathcal{F}$IFTY-FIVE

1-5 There was a man of the Pharisees, named Nicodemus, a ruler of the Jews:

2 The same came to Jesus by night, and said unto HIM, Rabbi we know that thou art a teacher come from God: for no man can do these miracles that thou doest, except God be with him.

3 Jesus answered and said unto him, Verily, verily I say unto thee, Except a man be born again, he cannot see the Kingdom of God.

Things of the Spirit enter a second time into his mother's womb and be born?

5 Jesus answered, Verily, verily I say unto thee, Except a man be born of the water and of the Spirit, he cannot enter into the Kingdom of God.

John 3: 1-5

This is one of the most amazing pieces of spiritual reality. You and I can be born for a second time. This does not make sense to the intellect of man. According to 1st Corinthians 2:14 …The natural man receiveth not the things of the Spirit of God: for they are foolishness unto him: neither can he know them, because they are spiritually discerned.

How is it that some people can get the Word of God, and understand it and others do not? Why do some read the Word of God, and they change their lives, and truly go from darkness to light? How do others transform from men and women of bitterness and hate, to the most loving of people? Why do some change, and others do not? Why do some change, and for a moment appear victorious, but later return to the mind of defeat and despair?

The key is in John 3: 1-5; some allow the Word of God to transform them, and they become a new creation (2nd Corinthians 5:17 and Jeremiah 18: 1-4). They become "Born Again" The first birth that we experience in a physical birth. We are born into the world with a sin nature, and all the flaws that this fallen world brings. Adam and Eve's sin is transferred into our ways of thinking and living. We react to everything from a natural perspective. When I feel like getting and staying angry, I get angry and stay angry. When I want to hate, I hate. When I want to gossip, I gossip. A little racism? (Here comes a sure road of defeat and bondage) Well, I was raised that way; to hate this group or that group, just because of how they look. You know, we spend so much time foolishly looking at race!! What if the hate was based on eye and not skin color? Some would then say, I hate those blue eyes, or I hate those green eyes. That sounds ridiculous doesn't it. They why do we have any issue with someone's skin color? That goes back to the satanic deception in the Garden of Eden. Hatred and bitterness, and evil were introduced to man at that time.

How then do we change from the things that have been sewn into us, that lead to our defeated life? We must be born again. We must be born again of the water and Spirit. According to John Chapter 1…We must be born again by the Word of God. We must accept HIS salvation. We surrender our lives to Jesus Christ, and let HIS Word in, and give HIS Word dominion. It is not just a "I accept Jesus", it is a "Jesus I surrender; please accept me" You must receive God's Word, and let HIS Spirit literally take possession of your spirit. You then notice that the unforgiveness, hatred, racism, bitterness, strife, envy and alike leave you. It is suddenly replaced with love, mercy, grace, kindness, gentleness. That is what truly being "Born Again will do.

Today…allow Jesus and HIS word to have HIS way in your life. Get "Born Again" of the Word of God, water, and Spirit, and watch your life miraculously change…God Bless.

*F*IFTY-SIX

15 That whosoever believeth in HIM should not perish, but have eternal life.

16 For God so loved the world, that HE gave HIS only begotten Son, that whosoever believeth in HIM should not perish, but have everlasting life.

17 For God sent not HIS Son into the world to condemn the world: but that the world through HIM might be saved.

John 3:15-17

We need to know how much God really loves us. He sent HIS only begotten Son. verses come alive, and bring us to an even more intimate walk with Jesus. 1st Timothy 3:16 says...And without controversy; great is the mystery of Godliness: God was manifest (revealed) in the flesh, justified in the Spirit, seen of angels, preached unto the Gentiles, believed on in the world, received up into glory.

This verse makes the only begotten Son become and incredibly loving act of God. The Son, is the Living God (who is a Spirit according to John 4:24) come in the flesh. An all loving Spirit, who needed a blood sacrifice to remove sin from the world. He put on flesh, became the Son of God, and died on the Cross of Calvary!! God so LOVED the world. God so loved you and me. God so loved the one you have difficulty forgiving. God so loved the one who said something evil about you, and HIS willingness to forgive was proven on the cross. !st Peter 2nd Chapter reminds us that Jesus Christ is our example. HE showed us the way to love

Since Jesus did not come into the world to condemn the world, we should not condemn one another. Since Jesus came with forgiveness and salvation as HIS mission, we should have love, grace, mercy and forgiveness as our mission. Jesus did come with love and forgiveness, and that is what we should do. Consider this…since Jesus opened the door for our sins to be removed, we then must forgive ALL offenses that come our way. That need to forgive is clearly laid out in Mark 11:25-26, and Matthew !8: 21-35. We must forgive, or we are not forgiven. Because God so loved us, we MUST love and forgive everyone. Please think of Jesus Christ's love for you, when offenses come your way.

Today…remember how much Jesus Christ loves you. Respond like Jesus to all offenses, always remembering HIS loving sacrifice on Calvary. God Bless.

$\mathcal{F}$IFTY-SEVEN

25 The other disciples therefore said unto him, We have seen the Lord. But he said unto them, Except I shall see in his hands the print of the nails, and put my finger in the print of the nails, and thrust my hand into his side, I will not believe.

26 And after eight days again, his disciples were within, and Thomas with them then came Jesus, the doors being shut and stood in the midst, and said, Peace be unto you.

27 Then saith HE to Thomas, Reach hither thy finger, and behold my hands; and reach hither thy hand, and thrust it into my side: and be not faithless but believing.

28 And Thomas answered and said unto Him, My Lord and My God.

29 And Jesus saith unto him, Thomas, because thou hast seen me, thou hast believed: Blessed are they that have not seen and yet believed.

John 20: 25-29

In John 20:25-29...Thomas identifies Jesus as God and says to Him. "My Lord and my God". Jesus never corrected Thomas for calling Him God... He corrected him for his unbelief. Jesus said " Blessed are ye who have not seen and yet believe...We are blessed because without seeing Jesus, we believe in Jesus. Jesus is Our Lord and Our God, and Our Savior. 1st John 5: 20 says...And we know that the Son of God has come, and has given us an understanding, that we may know Him that is true, and we are in Him that is true, even in His Son Jesus Christ. This is the true God and eternal life. Thomas had to see Jesus for himself to believe. We are truly blessed, because we do not see Him, yet we know that He is true. Jesus is the Son of

God, which literally means the "Flesh of God". He is the expressed image of the Invisible God of Abraham, Isaac, and Jacob. Jesus is my everything! He should be yours too. Think about the blessings that come into your life, for bowing your knees to Jesus; the King of Kings.

Since we are so blessed, then what are our responsibilities? We must tell the world about Jesus (Mark 16: 15-18). According to Hebrews 12:14, we must follow peace with all men and holiness, without which no man shall see the Lord. Because we are so blessed in Christ Jesus, we should walk in so much Agape love, that people literally ask us, "How can you love that person after what they did to you?" The world should be puzzled at our deaf ear to gossip; they should be amazed at our faithfulness. They should say what makes you different?

Today... since we know who Jesus is; My Lord and My God; since we believe on His marvelous name without seeing Him; let's tell the world about Him. Today, let's tell the world about Jesus with our words. Let's all show our confession by our actions...God bless.

$\mathcal{F}$IFTY-EIGHT

31 But they that wait upon the Lord shall renew their strength,
they shall renew their mount up with wings as eagles; they shall
run and not be weary, and they shall walk and not faint.

Isaiah 40: 31

7 Rest in the Lord, and wait patiently for HIM…

Psalm 37: 7(a)

Someone reading this today is in a major trial. You feel tired and weary. Lift your head, and look for your help. Psalm 121: 1-2 says…I will lift up mine eyes from whence cometh my help. My help cometh from the Lord, which made Heaven and Earth. Since you are in a battle, you might as well wait on your help. Jesus is your help. Jesus is my help. HE is the only true help that we have.

I want to make it abundantly clear to whoever is reading this daily devotion. I am in spiritual warfare. I am in the fight. I need Jesus. I know that few times in this book that I will reiterate that my fight against satan is personal. He is a liar, and a thief, and has stolen many things from me and many of you. He has attacked my family, my finances, and my health. I have had to trust that Jesus will come by and visit my fight and help me. I have had to wait on HIM. When I quote Isaiah 40:31, it is from experience. I often have get help to hold on to this. The Book of Proverbs reminds us that iron sharpens iron. We sometimes need someone to remind us how wise and profitable it is to wait on the Lord. He will strengthen you during the fight. He will keep your arms up, just the way Aaron and Hur held up the arms of Moses. You may be in the fight of your life. I understand what you are going through. JESUS STILL LOVES YOU VERY, VERY MUCH.

Today…keep your eyes on Jesus through any struggle that you are in. Wait on the Lord; let HIM strengthen you. He will bring you the victory, and strengthen you through the wait…God Bless.

$\mathcal{F}$IFTY-NINE

6 And ye shall hear of wars and rumours of wars: see that ye be
not troubled: for all these things must come to pass, but the end
is not yet.

Matthew 24 :6

In Matthew 24:6 Jesus forewarned us that everything that we see in the news is part of the plan. HE said that wars and rumors of wars must come to pass. Matthew 24 is an end time breakdown of prophetic events. Verse 7 says that nation shall rise against nation, and kingdom against kingdom. Both verses in Matthew 24 remind us that these are just the beginning of sorrows, and the end is not yet. Verse 6 says...BE NOT TROUBLED. When you see the famines, diseases, earthquakes, and the flooding of terrible storms, we are watching more of Matthew 24 being fulfilled. The events of North Korea and the Middle East confirm the verse 6, 7 and 8 warnings of Matthew 24. Here are some of the critical signs...verse 9-14 remind us that many will be hated, just for saying they love Jesus. Iniquity and bitterness will take over, and the love of many shall grow cold. People will not forgive. We also know that one of the key signs of these end times is the re-birth of Israel in 1948. This fulfilled Ezekiel 37:1-14, that described Israel as coming back to life. Then in Matthew 24:14...we see that the Gospel of Jesus Christ must be preached to the entire world. That is OUR job, and given the events of the day, this must be a priority. We MUST love, forgive...forgive and love. The news and scripture confirm not the end of the world, but the soon return of Jesus Christ. We must read this chapter with urgency. Never...Never let your love grow cold... always forgive. Let's not be ashamed of The Gospel of Jesus Christ.

Today... know what time it is based on events and these scriptures. Let's prepare for the return of Jesus... given the times... let's reveal that we are HIS... God bless.

$\mathcal{S}$IXTY

8 The grass withereth, and the flower fadeth : but the Word of our
God shall stand forever.

Isaiah 40: 8

24 For all flesh is as grass, and all the glory of man as the flower
of grass. The grass withereth, and the thereof falleth away.

25 But the Word of the Lord endureth forever. And this is the Word
which by the Gospel is preached unto you.

1ˢᵗ Peter 1:24-25

These scriptures I find to be encouraging, and help build confidence. If I am going through a trial or situation, what I put my faith in seriously matters. Do I stand on a rock, or do I stand on sand. According to Jesus, storms are coming into ALL of our lives. There is no exception; it rains on the just and the unjust (Matthew 5:45). In Matthew 7: 24-29, Jesus said that a wise man builds his house on a rock. The Rock is Jesus; the sure foundation is the Word of God. Jesus said that a foolish man builds his house on sand, and great is the fall of that house.

The Word of God is an absolute place of victory for those who put their trust in it. I have called on God's Word when I needed a healing, and Jesus healed me. You see, Jesus healed me from cancer. No one can convince me that Jesus cannot heal. The Word of God spoke again and again of Jesus miracle healings. As a cancer survivor, I am glad that I stood on the Word of God, and not the diagnosis. Cancer was REALLY there! The Word of God was there too, and the cancer was defeated. I have been healed by the laying on of hands, and I have been healed in an operating room, with the help of a physician. Either way…Jesus gets the glory for my healing. The healing is in HIS Word, and HIS Word stands forever.

I saw miracles happen in my family through some of the darkest obstacles and struggles. I remember praying when I had a major financial need, and reminded God of HIS Word. I said to the Lord, but you said in your Word in Luke 6:38...Give and it shall be given to you. Good measure, pressed down and shaken together, shall men give into your bosom. The phone rang when I got off of my knees. It was a friend who offered to give me everything that I needed to meet the need.

The Word of God reminds us in 1st Timothy 2:4 and 2nd Peter 3:9 that Jesus wants all men to be saved. My grandparents prayed for their rebellious hard headed grandson (me). I was saved before my grandmother went home to be with the Lord. The Word stands forever. Her prayers and fastings for me were a sweet smelling savor to the Lord.

Today...Trust God at HIS wonderful awesome Word. You can trust HIS Word. Believe God for HIS miracles. Jesus is a Rock, and a sure foundation... God Bless.

SIXTY-ONE

30 He must increase, but I must decrease.

John 3:30

5 Likewise, ye younger, submit yourselves unto the elder. Yea, all of you be subject one to another, and be clothed with humility: for God resisteth the proud, and giveth grace to the humble.

1ˢᵗ Peter 5:5

14 The Lord upholdeth all that fall, and raiseth up all those that be bowed down.

Do you want to get God's attention today? DECREASE !! Jesus makes HIS Word clear…He raises those who humble themselves. HE blesses those who take a humble road. God put wicked King Manasseh back on the throne in Judah when he humbled himself. King Ahab in Israel was equally wicked. When he humbled himself before the Prophet Elijah, God told Elijah to tell Ahab that HIS fierce wrath would not come on Ahab, but on the next generation.

Now a prophet that Jesus said was the "Greatest Born to Women", John the Baptist, said in John 3:30…He (Jesus) must increase, and I must decrease. This great Jewish prophet new that Messiah Jesus had come, He knew that he had to lower his position, his presence and ministry, to allow Jesus glory to fully be known. We need to do the same, and realize that for Jesus to fully get the glory in our lives, WE MUST DECREASE!! We must put our will and position aside for the Glory of God to be revealed. It frankly, is not about me…IT IS ABOUT JESUS!!

Grace is the unmerited favor of God. We get it through humility…we get when we forgive those who hurt and offend us. God's unchangeable word reminds us again and again that grace come with humility and repentance.

**I have personally seen Jesus fix a situation in my life, the moment that I recognized that pride was trying to creep into my spirit. Let me honestly tell you that I was trying to work out some financial matters (a problem that I and many others have had on a regular basis...we need to be honest in this arena). Things began to work out in my favor. I actually thought how wonderful it was that "I" was working things out. The moment that "I" entered into the equation, things began to sour quickly. A check that I was expecting did not come. The accounts began to have issues. Then, Jesus sent me conviction about the pride that was trying to get in. I will not give satan on bit of credit. I can be foolish enough on my own. I repented, decreased, got humble, and told Jesus that the glory completely belongs to HIM. My check came the same day that I repented.

Pride may be the one thing keeping you today from what you have been crying out to the Lord for. Pride will keep you from recognizing the power of forgiving someone else. Please remember Mark 11:25-26; if we do not forgive, we are not forgiven. Pride keeps us from decreasing, forgiving, and walking in true repentance.

Today...please kick pride out of your mind and spirit. Decrease and exalt Jesus in your life. Humble yourself, forgive, love, and watch Jesus anoint and bless your life...God Bless.

SIXTY-TWO

16 And he answered, Fear not: for they that be with us are more that they that be with them.

17 And Elisha prayed and said, Lord I pray thee, open his eyes that he may see. And the Lord opened the eyes of the young man; and he saw: and, behold the mountain was full of horses and chariots of fire, round about Elisha.

2nd Kings 6:16-17

6 Ye are of God little children and have overcome them; for greater is He that is in you than he that is in the world.

1st John 4:6

Don't give up today, you are not alone. When the world, stands against you; when you stand with Jesus, you are in the majority. You may be challenged by those who mock you, Jesus, and everything righteous. Believe me; they will appear to be winning, and you sometimes frankly just look like a very weak "chump" standing for Christ against this multitude. Words do hurt, and hurtful actions can break your spirit. You can be made to feel that somehow we are a lesser person for saying Jesus is Lord, and I stand for HIS righteousness.

The situation that Elisha faced in 2nd Kings 6 was a lot like what we face. He and his servant were surrounded by a large troop. The servant began to panic as we do with bad news. Elisha had seen Elijah carried off into heaven and knew the angelic host and the chariots of fire are real. He said in verse 16...Open the eyes of my servant, that he may there are more with us than with them... 1st John 4:6 says...Ye are of God little children and have overcome them...for greater is He that is in you than he that is in the world. God cannot lie and does not change. HE showed Himself mighty for Elisha, and his servant. HE said 14 times in the Book of Hebrews the word "better", describing our New Testament relationship to God over the Old Testament. We have the complete Word of God, the Holy Ghost on the inside, the Blood of Jesus, and HIS mighty name, to help us defeat satan, and evil voices and actions,

Today...Open your eyes and look on Jesus... The author and finisher of our faith....as HE delivered Elisha...so will HE deliver us today... God bless

SIXTY-THREE

14 And the priest shall take some of the blood of the trespass offering, and the priest shall put it upon the tip of the right ear of him that is to be cleansed, and upon the thumb of his right hand, and upon the great toe of his right foot...

Leviticus 14:14

11 For the life of the flesh is in the blood: and I have given it to you upon the altar to make an atonement for your souls, for it is the blood that maketh atonement for the soul.

Leviticus 17:11

22 And almost all things are by the law purged with blood: and without the shedding of blood is no remission.

Hebrews 9: 22

The first time I read this scripture in Leviticus 14, I instantly saw an amazing piece of understanding in the Word. The Word of God is read line upon line, and precept upon precept; here a little, there a little (Isaiah 28). Scripture to scripture, Genesis to Revelation, it is truly about Jesus. The blood placed on the head, hand, and toe of him that is to be cleansed, very clearly shows where Jesus would bleed from. Why is that important? The Old and New Testament show how important the crucifixion really is. Hebrews 9: 22 tells us without the shedding of blood, sin cannot be remitted or removed.

I can be at my lowest point, and some lonely, hurting days, I can be; and suddenly I think about the cross. I remember the Crown of Thorns, the nails in Jesus' hands and feet. I suddenly put my pain into perspective. No matter what has been done to me; it does not compare to what Jesus suffered. Because Jesus made that awesome sacrifice, my sins are forgiven. I am guaranteed eternal life in HIM. Leviticus 17:11 reminds me that the life is in the blood. Please don't let satan overwhelm you with negative thought.

You may have faced attack from many people, even those closest to you. If you can keep your mind on the blood, the sacrifice on the cross, and the eternal life that the blood of Jesus brought you, you can pray and intercede for those who hurt you. The blood on the head, hand, and toe is a picture of Jesus on the cross. The thought of Jesus on the cross, and HIS shed blood had kept me hopeful, again, again, and again. This blood covenant with me (I make it personal) reminds of Jesus Agape, perfect love. John 15:13 says Greater love have no man than this; that a man lay down his life for his friends. Jesus laid down HS life for me. The Cross remains the symbol of my hope of God's awesome promises.

Today...remember the Blood of Jesus and HIS awesome loving sacrifice on the Cross. It was done for you, to remove your sin, give you eternal life, and a great reference point to look upon as life gets tough...God Bless.

SIXTY-FOUR

9 Hide thy face from my sins, and blot out all my iniquities.

10 Create in me a clean heart, O God: and renew a right spirit within me.

17 The sacrifices of God are a broken spirit: a broken and a contrite heart, O God, thou will not despise.

Psalm 51: 9-10 & 17

Who has done something wrong? All of us have! Romans 3: 23 reminds us that All have sinned and come short of the Glory of God. I am trying today to remove all of our self-denial and self-righteousness. Isaiah 64:6 says that All our righteousness is as filthy rags. We have stubbed our toe, and said something that we should not. We have lied, gotten terribly angry, looked at something on TV or the computer that we should not have. We have said that we will be there at 7, and arrived at 8 (this is certainly me). We all have sinned. ** We have said, " I forgive you" and really did not. This is one of the most common sins in church, since WE commonly forget Mark 11: 25-26 (if we do not forgive, we are not forgiven).

I we have done all these things, when we look at the Word of God, we see the very same shortcomings and failures. We see Paul and Barnabas have a terrible argument. Paul was unmerciful over John Mark's shortcomings and did not want to take him on a missionary journey. God literally had to bring Paul to repentance over this before he died (read 2nd Timothy 4). Peter said he would die with Jesus, and denied HIM 3 times. Hezekiah stopped giving to the Lord, and was told that he was going to die. He repented with tears, and God gave him 15 more years (read Isaiah Chapter 38). Jehoshaphat continually associated with negative people and corrupted his family. He was called a righteous man in the Word of God.

In Psalm 51, King David was in a very bad place. He gave in to lust (very common in our visually lustful culture). David had also allowed himself to become spiritually lax, and did not go to battle with the armies of Israel. He was walking on the roof, and spotted Bathsheba, who was taking a bath. He not only ended up committing adultery with Bathsheba, but had her husband Urijah killed on the battlefield. David wrote Psalm 51 and 32 as a heart-felt repentance. ** David did not justify self, or make excuses. He wrote in verse 10…Create in me a clean heart. He cried out to God in verse 9, and said, "Blot out my iniquities". If you read 2nd Samuel 14th chapter, when Nathan the Prophet confronts David about his sin, David said that he sinned against the Lord. Nathan told David that he was forgiven. God forgave David instantly, knowing that his heart was genuine, and his repentance was real. David cried…Create in me a clean heart.

When Jesus sees a broken heart and a contrite spirit, HE moves HIS mercy over our sins. Since we all have sinned, we need this mercy. David had done much evil, but recognized his sin. He was forgiven, and the blood line of Jesus, still came through him. ** By the way, God did not remove David from the throne.

Today…recognize that you and I have sinned. We all need to cry out to the Lord, say like David…Create in me a clean heart, and renew a right spirit within me…God Bless.

SIXTY-FIVE

6 But we are all as an unclean thing, and all our righteousnesses are as filthy rags; and we all do fade as a leaf; and our iniquities, like the wind, have taken us away.

Isaiah 64 :6

Why would I love a verse that says...We are all as an unclean thing? Why do I love the Isaiah 64: 6 proclamation that...All of our Righteousness is as filthy rags? Jesus puts ALL us on an even playing field. John 3:1-7 we must be born again in Jesus. Ephesians 2:8-9 says...by grace are ye saved through faith; it is the gift of God, not of works, lest any man should boast. I cannot do a checklist of 10 or 15 or 20 works to know that I am going to Heaven. That is an awesome truth. How would I ever know if I did enough works. How would I know if my works are good enough? Isaiah 64:6 says...my own righteousness is as filthy rags. I cannot do it my way (with apologies to Mr. Sinatra). My way...my works...my Righteousness does not get me in the door. IT IS THE BLOOD OF JESUS CHRIST THAT OPENS THE HEAVENLY DOOR. Revelation 12:11 says that we overcome by the Blood of the Lamb.

I don't work my way in; I come to Jesus with humble repentance and faith. Psalm 51 says we need a broken heart and contrite spirit. We bow a knee to Jesus...by faith. We look to the cross and remember HIS shed Blood. Jesus shed Blood for us is the cleanest most awesome thing in the world. The works of love, mercy and Forgiveness comes after I am in Jesus.

Today... remember that my works don't get me in the door. Overcome everything with the key to the door of Victory...the Blood of Jesus... God bless.

$\mathcal{S}$IXTY-SIX

12 And because iniquity shall abound, the love of many shall wax cold.

13 But he that shall endure to the end, the same shall be saved.
Matthew 24: 12-13

These verses make it very clear what time we are in spiritually. The 24th Chapter of Matthew is a sermon preached on the Mount of Olives to HIS disciples. Jesus' disciples spoke to HIM, and spoke to the wonder and beauty of the Temple. Jesus immediately told them that the Temple would be completely torn down (Not one stone left on another v.2). This prophecy was fulfilled in 70 A.D. The rest of the chapter is dedicated to events that will affect Jews and Gentiles in the end times.

Jesus described what is taking place in today's culture in verse 12; The love of many (most) shall wax (or become) cold. HE stated clearly that iniquity shall abound. Iniquity is the inner darkness, that leads us to the sinful acts of hatred, bitterness, strife and unforgiveness. When iniquity takes over, the love is drowned out by the inner darkness. The evidence of verse 12 is clear. Families are breaking up every day. Children are running away; husbands are leaving wives; wives are leaving husbands. Churches are going through internal turmoil. People will leave if the message preached isn't satisfactory. There are fights over who sits in what seat, or who gets what parking space. Many will leave Jesus Christ, and fulfil the prophecy in 2nd Thessalonians 2:3, which states that there will be a great falling away.

Matthew 24:13 gives us the answer that we ALL must strive to achieve… Endurance. Jesus said, He that endures to the end will be saved. He that does not quit will make it. Those who stay in the Agape love of Jesus Christ, will make it. Those who reject the hatred and bitterness will endure. Those who keep their vows will endure. **Those who forgive unconditionally will endure, and when Jesus comes for HIS church, they will be caught up to meet the Lord in the air (1Thessalonians 4: 13-18), and forever will be with Jesus.

Today…Keep the love in and bitterness and iniquity out. Let Jesus keep your heart and mind in HIS love, always being very mindful of the prophetic time that we are in… God Bless.

$\mathcal{S}$IXTY-SEVEN

12 Fight the good fight of faith, lay hold on eternal life, where unto thou art also called, and hast professed a good profession before many witnesses.

1st Timothy 6:12

^{3}Thou therefore endure hardness, as a good soldier of Jesus Christ.

^{4} No man that warreth entangleth himself with the affairs of this life; that he may please him who hath chosen him to be a soldier
2nd Timothy 3: 3-4

There are some things in life worth fighting for. We can get ourselves entangled in all of the bitter, hateful rhetoric of our time. We can find ourselves debating whose life matters over someone else's (this thought is 100% contrary to Jesus teaching, as HE died for ALL people). What are you fighting for? What matters to you? What happened to…For God so loved the world? You would this that the Word of God reads…For God so loved this group; but not that group. What is important to you? What are you fighting for? Is it the good fight of faith, that leads to eternal life?

We were recently watching a video presentation about the Church in China. The saints there are suffering immense persecution. They have to worship under extreme conditions. There are hundreds, sometimes thousands crammed into standing room only settings. Their services sometimes last for 12 hours. They just want more Jesus. That's what they are fighting for. Their fight is for eternal things, the saving of souls, reaching the lost, ministering to hurting people. Truly, there is no time for them to be divided, and worry about who took my parking place or my favorite seat in church.

Jesus spoke to of Books of Remembrance in Revelation Chapter 20. The Books are there basically as a record of our works. The same chapter in

Revelation also mentions the Book of life. The names of the redeemed are in the Book of Life. The unrighteous acts of man are judged out of the Books. What are you fighting for today? I do not want those that I love in the Books; I want them in the "Book". I do not want an enemy in the Books. I want them saved, on their way to Heaven, and their names written in the Book (Read Revelation 20:10-15). That is something truly worth fighting for. What are you fighting for? What are you entangled in today? Paul called us soldiers in Jesus 'Army. Soldier…What are you fighting for today?

Today…Fight for the things that yield an eternal reward. Fight to bring people to a saving knowledge of the King of Kings and Lord of Lords…Jesus Christ.

SIXTY-EIGHT

1 The Spirit of the Lord GOD is upon me; because the LORD hath anointed me to preach good tidings unto the meek; He hath sent me to bind up the brokenhearted, to proclaim liberty to the captives, and the opening of the prison to them that are bound

Isaiah 61:1

This prophecy refers to the coming mission of Jesus. He was coming with the Spirit of God upon HIM. He was coming to bring good tidings to man, and a hope that had never been in the earth before. The poor would hear of the Glory of God, the blind eyes opened, the lame to walk, and the deaf to hear. Man, would finally be set free from the one thing that kept him in bondage...sin.

In Luke 4, Jesus came into the synagogue, and read the Isaiah 61 passage, as was the custom on the Sabbath day. HE then closed the reading, and said...This day is this scripture fulfilled in your ears (verse 21). He read the passage after fasting 40 days and defeating the devil by denying HIMSELF, and speaking the Word of God. HE moved forward in power and might in HIS earthly ministry.

This scripture has a lot of very practical application for anything that you are going through right now. You need to know that Jesus Christ's power is well able to help you, and that right early. I am in some tough situations RIGHT NOW. Many of you who read this are in some tough situations RIGHT NOW. Jesus said in the scripture that HE will bind the brokenhearted, and bring liberty to the captives. We may be captives to depression, or anger, or unforgiveness. We may be brokenhearted over family rejection. Since Jesus was betrayed by one of HIS own disciples, HE knows how to comfort and help you through your time of hurt or abandonment. When you in financial trouble, and you call on Jesus for help, remember that HE told Peter to cast a line, and the fish that he brought up, had gold in his mouth to pay the taxes for both of them. Jesus was anointed to bring victory in all these areas of our lives. **The greatest gift that Jesus brings us is the saving of our souls.

Today...count on Jesus for your salvation, and for comfort, healing, and help in all of your life trials...God Bless.

$\mathcal{S}$IXTY-NINE

1 Therefore thou art inexcusable O man, whosoever thou art that judgest: for wherein thou judgest another, thou condemnest thyself; for thou that judgest doest the same things.

2 But we are sure that the judgement of God is according to truth against them which commit such things.

3 And thinkest thou this O Man, that judgest them which do such things, and doest the same, that thou shall escape the judgement of God?

4 Or despises thou the riches of HIS goodness and forebearance and longsuffering; not knowing that the goodness of God leadeth thee to repentance?

Romans 2:1-4

Jesus told us in Matthew 7: 1, Judge not, that ye be not judged. Verse 2 reminds us with the same mercy that you give, will be the same mercy that you receive. Romans 2:1-4 should make us stop and think about how we treat the weakness and shortcomings of others. If I see a weakness in you, that is my call to pray and intercede for your deliverance. If I have the love of Jesus Christ in me (and this WILL be tried) I pray for my weak brother or sister. I do not agree with the sin, if I try to restore someone to righteousness. I am demonstrating love by restoring my brother or sister to Jesus (Galatians 6:1-2) and praying for them.

My personal responsibility in this scripture is clear...examine myself, and consider where I stand; do not judge or condemn another. This again, does not mean that I give someone a pass, however if I consider MY OWN SIN, I come to a place where I remember the goodness that Jesus has given me. HE did not kick me out of HIS Kingdom for my anger or lust. If I become self-righteous or prideful, or hard hearted, I can't wait to put my finger on someone else. REMEMBER MATTHEW 7:1-2...THE LEVEL OF MERCY THAT YOU GIVE, DIRECTLY RELATES TO THE LEVEL OF MERCY THAT YOU GIVE. YOU GIVE NO MERCY...YOU GET NO MERCY!!

This is something that I must relay to married people; you made a vow! Now your spouse has had a weakness or a fall. You focus on their betrayal and adultery. You are convinced that you do not have to forgive, and your bitterness is justified. What happens next is usually that you find voices of negativity to justify your bitterness. Then comes the divorce. ** May I humbly ask you a question? How many times have you lusted after someone else, and imagined an intimate encounter with someone other than your spouse? Jesus said in Matthew 5:27-28 that if you look on a woman with lustful imagination, you have committed adultery in your heart already. You see, Romans 2:1 says that you have no excuse when you judge another, and do the same thing. Who are you going to believe? Will you believe your angry friend, or Jesus; The King of Kings?

Please do not dismiss what is clearly a needed word in the times that we live in now. It all about judgement, and a lack of love, mercy, and forgiveness. This is the time to stop destroying families, and making our children believe that God is not real. Please do not say that you don't understand. I DO understand, and I have one response to all of the hurt, pain, and rejection. **FORGIVE EVERYBODY FOR EVERYTHING!! Matthew 18th Chapter reminds us of the man who was forgiven for much, and did not forgive. He found himself in the same prison that the king had unconditionally released him from.

Today...Consider yourself, and everything that you and I have done wrong. Forgive all things completely, remembering that the level of mercy that you give, is the level of mercy that you measure out (or lack thereof) will come back to your door...God Bless.

$\mathcal{S}$EVENTY

1 Brethren, if a man be overtaken in a fault, ye which are spiritual, restore such an one in the spirit of meekness; considering thyself, lest thou also be tempted.

2 Bear ye one another's burdens, and so fulfil the law of Christ.

3 For if a man think himself to be something, when he is nothing, he deceiveth himself.

I did not serve in the United States Military. I did however serve 29 years in law enforcement, as a sworn officer and detective. I served 16 years searching for the missing children of Montgomery County, Maryland. There are a few life lessons that I learned, that line up with this scripture. I pray that you can follow my thought process, because I see these verses like a military battle buddy, or a brother officer, or that missing child that you go to great lengths to recover. In Galatians 6, the Apostle Paul wrote…if a brother be overtaken in a fault, you who are spiritual restore that person. You must consider yourself, lest ye also be tempted. If you refuse to restore that person, it should be of no surprise that no one reaches a hand to recover you at your point of weakness.

I had an awesome partner for 13 years during my time as a detective. She and I would often talk about life, object lessons were kind of a regular part of our discussions. I would frequently use war movies as a source of my examples. A particular war movie chronicled the life of a contentious objector, who won the Medal of Honor, without picking up a rifle. His absolute missing was to rescue his wounded comrades, and get them to safety. I view Galatians 6 the same way. We who are strong should have the mind to restore our spiritually wounded brother or sister. We need to carry them across the finish line to Heaven. This does not mean that I compromise what I spiritually know to be right, however it means that I move in prayer, fasting, and a word to help that weak saint get the mind to repent. This also fulfill 1st Timothy 2:4 and 2nd Peter 3:9, that remind us that Jesus wants all to be saved, and come to repentance.

Today...remember how loving and merciful that Jesus has been with you. He went to great lengths to save and/or recover you. We should reach out in love to recover the overtaken, wounded brother or sister, and bring them back to Jesus...God Bless.

$\mathcal{S}$EVENTY-ONE

26 The servant fell down and worshipped him and said, Lord have patience, and I will pay thee all.

27 The lord of that servant was moved with compassion, and loosed him and forgave him the debt.

28 But the same servant went out and found one his fellow servants, which owed him a hundred pence: and he laid hands on him, and took him by the throat saying, Pay me what thou owest.

29 And his fellowservant fell down and besought him saying, Have patience with me and I will pay thee all.

30 And he would not: but went and cast him into prison, till he should pay the debt.

32 Then his lord, after that he had called him, said unto him, O thou wicked servant, I forgave thee all that debt, because thou desirest me:

33 Shouldest not thou have had compassion on thy fellowservant even as I had pity on thee?

34 And his lord delivered him to the tormenters, till he should pay all that was due unto him.

Matthew 18:26-30; 32-34

This remains the single biggest challenge to the church!! These verses in Matthew 18:21-35 record a conversation with Jesus and the disciples. Peter asked how often should he forgive his brother; SEVEN TIMES IN A DAY? When Jesus answered Peter, and told him that he must forgive SEVENTY

TIMES SEVEN IN A DAY. Could you imagine someone offending you 490 times in a day? It really is not possible. That number is renewed every day, because Lamentations 3:23 reminds us that the mercy of God is NEW every morning.

Consider the servant in this passage of scripture, who owed his lord 10,000 talents. I have read several differing views of how much money that is. I have read estimates that the number is near 10 million dollars. This is not a debt that frankly can ever be repaid; and that is the point. We owe Jesus an unpayable debt, that we are not able to repay. ** Jesus paid a debt that HE DID NOT OWE ON THE CROSS. The servant fell on his face, and cried out for mercy. He and his wife, and children, along with their possessions were going to be sold to pay his debt. Take a minute before you think that this servant is not you or me...IT IS!! Romans 6:23 says for the wages (payment) for sin is death, but the gift of God is eternal life through Jesus Christ our Lord. Romans 3:23 reminds us that ALL have sinned and come short of the Glory of God.

Seventy times seven is our requirement with forgiving others. There is no exception. None of us can say, "You don't know what he, she, or they did!". Remember that the debt that you owe for everything that you have done wrong was paid by Jesus. The servant who had been forgiven for 10,000 talents, went and threw a fellow servant in prison who owed him a hundred pence. Again, I have read different estimates on this amount. It is approximately 3 months' wages, and is a very payable debt. 10,000 talents cannot be repaid; 100 pence can. Our sin could not be removed, except for the precious Blood of Jesus, that cleanses us from all sin, when we ask HIM. HIS BLOOD TIPS THE SCALES IN OUR FAVOR!

The servant who was forgiven, had one responsibility...forgive others. This is also confirmed in Mark 11: 25-26. Jesus said in those passages of scripture that if we do not forgive...WE ARE NOT FORGIVEN. The servant had been forgiven, but forgot the mercy given to him. When we do not forgive, we are like that servant, forgetting that we were lost sinners (born into that status due to Adam's fall). We have been given a sin nature, and no one ever had to teach us to sin; we just did it. Now since we are ALL guilty, we must forgive everybody...everything...all the time. ** This is not the "I forgive,

but don't forget lie". This true forgiveness, must be like Jesus' forgiveness...
IT NEVER HAPPENED !!

Do you want Jesus to hold on to your offenses? I do not, and I am determined to make it to Heaven. I am not there yet, and take nothing for granted. SEVENTY TIMES SEVEN, AND IT DID NOT HAPPEN,

I spent years in bitter hatred and misery after the death of my brother Jay in 1981. He was killed at the hands of a drunk driver. For years, I simply did not forgive, and then the man who killed him was arrested for DUI again, in the station where I was assigned. I drove to the station, full of anger. I am certain that my intentions were not good. I was a 350-pound powerlifter, and had very evil thoughts of what I wanted to do to this man. The arresting officer, was Officer Erik Tammaru; nor Pastor Erik Tammaru; a true Man of God. He saw my anger, and took on a very powerful boldness. He told me directly that if I do not forgive him; God would not forgive me. I was nor "Born-Again" yet, but thank Jesus for parents who took me to church, and grandparents who fasted and prayed for my soul. The fear of God suddenly gripped me, and I could not touch the man. ** I have since truly forgiven him, and that is very liberating to me, and pleasing to Jesus.

Today...remember that you and I owe 10,000 talents, and our LORD Jesus will forgive any and all offenses, if we come to him humbly by faith, and receive HIS loving pardon. We must then forgive ANY and ALL offenses... SEVENTY TIMES SEVEN EVERYDAY...God Bless.

SEVENTY-TWO

13 Then were there brought unto him little children, that he should put his hands on them, and pray: and the disciples rebuked them.

14 But Jesus said, Suffer little children and forbid them not to come unto me: for of such is the Kingdom of Heaven.

Matthew 19: 13-14

There is a true way to come to Jesus...like a child. When the disciples were approached, and asked if the children could be brought to Jesus, and blessed by the Master, the disciples stopped them. Frankly, If I were a parent at that time, and I saw the true power of Jesus, with blind eyes opening and the dead being raised, I would definitely want Jesus to lay hands and bless my child. After Jesus corrected HIS disciples, He told them that the example of the Kingdom of Heaven, is the child-like nature of a child. Jesus said for of such is the Kingdom of Heaven.

When Jesus used the example of the children's child-like nature, HE was illustrating an important point. A child will follow; a child is generally very forgiving, and frankly does not hate after parental correction. We adults tends to take on the character of victimhood, and take EVERYTHING personally. Child-like faith believes the parental voice of direction and instruction. This is not "childish", as we have all seen our children fight over toys, or grow up to receive evil communication, and become rebellious. Jesus was referring to a tender heart of a child, that believes, and can follow the shepherdly voice of a loving parent. Notice how the disciples missed the heart of God in this matter. It is not an uncommon error. We make the statement..." I am Grown". When we tell Jesus all about OUR level of adulthood, we are on our way to the experiences and correction, that will show us that we need to get back to "Child-like" faith and character.

Today...let us purpose to return to a tender, child-like heart; for of such is the kingdom of Heaven...God Bless.

$\mathcal{S}$EVENTY-THREE

21 Fear not, O land; be glad and rejoice: for the Lord will do great things.

Joel 2:21

15 And he said, Hearken ye all Judah, and ye inhabitants of Jerusalem, and thou King Jehoshaphat. Thus saith the Lord unto you, Be not afraid or dismayed by reason of this great multitude: for the battle is not yours, but God's.

17 Ye shall not need to fight in this battle: set yourselves, stand ye still and see the salvation of the Lord with you, O Judah and Jerusalem: fear not, nor be dismayed: tomorrow go out against them: for the Lord will be with you.

2nd Chronicles 20:15 & 17

Who is facing a great multitude today? I am, and many of you are. We have seen the Goliaths of sickness and physical pain, betrayal, family discord, financial troubles, oppression, depression, and sometimes just general life frustration. The Goliaths are huge, just like the giant in 1st Samuel 17. Goliath may have been 9 feet tall, but David still slew him, with mighty help from an all-powerful mighty God. Israel was going through times of great trouble, when the Prophet Joel was ministering. In the midst of trouble, God spoke through Joel, and said "Fear not, O land; be GLAD and rejoice, for the Lord will do great things. Someone needs to know today, that Jesus is a "hands-on" God, who truly does intervene and help in our lives.

In 2009, I was at a doctor appointment, and was preparing to walk out of the office. I had a lab slip, and suddenly, I turned and asked my doctor for a PSA test. I was really too young to be concerned with Prostate Cancer. My lab result revealed an elevated number. We followed up with further test, and cancer was discovered. I was treated, but I TRULY GIVE JESUS ALL

OF THE GLORY, FOR THE DETECTION OF MY CANCER, AND MY EVENTUAL COMPLETE HEALING. HE did great things.

In 2nd Chronicles 20, Judah and Jerusalem were surrounded by three enemies. They were outnumbered about 10 to 1. King Jehoshaphat called for prayer and fasting, which is a true weapon given to the church in Matthew 17. He then cried out to the Lord, and reminded HIM of HIS Word, and promises. The Word came back to King Jehoshaphat, and victory was proclaimed. He was told the battle is not yours but God's. Someone truly needs to read this today, and I know that I am receiving encouragement through a tough time in my life by writing it.

When the Children of Judah prepared to go out to battle, they had already been told that they have the victory. They were told to believe the prophets, and they shall prosper. They used an amazing battle plan (one we need to use as well through the fight). They sent the singers out to praise the Lord, for the Beauty of Holiness. When they found the armies of Ammon, Moab, and Mount Seir, they were all dead. The armies warred against each other. Judah gathered up the spoil, and praised the Lord all the way back.

I do not know what you are going through right now, but if your battle is anything like mine, you see Goliath, you see the armies of Ammon, Moab, and Mount Seir. They are just disguised today as a rebellious or runaway child, an unfaithful spouse, the loss of a job, turmoil in your church (the gates of hell will not prevail), great financial difficulty, or other issues of life. Jesus has led you and I to the shore of the Red Sea, to show Pharaoh, who the True God is. The battle is not yours, but God's. I was actually told this very thing by several very anointed people, when a major trial in my life began. ** Jesus wants this fight David' HE wants your Goliath; HE wants to do great things. ** HE deserves ALL of the glory when HE does.

Today…know that the same God who fought for Judah and Jerusalem, wants to help you today. HE is well able to bring victory in the time of need…God Bless.

SEVENTY-FOUR

1 Behold how good and how pleasant it is for Brethren to dwell together in unity.

3 As the dew of Hermon, and as the dew that descended from the mountains of Zion: for there the Lord commanded the blessing, even life forevermore.

Psalm 133: 1 & 3

25 And Jesus knew their thoughts and said unto them, Every kingdom divided against itself is brought to desolation; and every city or house divided against itself shall not stand;

Matthew 12: 25

Unity brings victory…Division brings defeat. Jesus was having a discussion with the hard-hearted, religious Pharisees (as HE often did attempting to put life into their dead, dry hearts and minds). They saw HIS power, and accused Jesus of casting out satan by the power of satan. Jesus immediately told them a truth for the spiritual realm, and the natural. A kingdom divided against itself cannot stand. There is no unity. Jesus, of course as God manifested in the flesh, demonstrated that he had ALL power over satan. HE also made it clear that unity brings blessing, while division leads to defeat.

My high school football team got off to a terrible start in my senior year. We had a 1-3 record. One of our coaches, Ken Rippetoe had a talk with us after the loss. He did not yell or scream. He simply told us that we were not unified, and were not playing to our potential. Friends, that speech was given to the Northwood football team in 1979. I am writing this in 2017. Those words have remained with me all of these years. We finished with a 6-4 record, recorded 5 shut-out wins, and were one very bad call from going 7-3 and winning our division. What was the key…UNITY.

In Psalm 133, David wrote that it is good and pleasant for brothers and sisters to dwell in unity. Verse 3 says that where God sees unity, HE commands the blessing. When God commands the blessing, NOTHING, BUT NOTHING CAN STOP IT !! All power in Heaven and earth is unleashed to move on our behalf. Why? Because Jesus sees unity and agreement. We must agree with HIS Word, and the leading of HIS Spirit. The Spirit of Christ leads us to repent from sin, trust God's Word, and walk in humility and forgiveness. Division and discord hinder a move of God. In fact, In Proverbs 6: 15-19, we see things that God truly hates. HE is God, and when HE is displeased with something, HE will let us know, so that we can repent. He calls the sowing of discord among brethren an abomination. Why? Discord breaks up unity, hinders blessing, and robs the faith of some; especially new converts to Christ.

Today...Let us all get to a mind and spirit of UNITY. First, with the Word of God, the love of God, and Spirit of God. Then, let us unify one with another, and watch Jesus perform HIS miracles in our lives...God Bless.

SEVENTY-FIVE

19 God is not a man, that HE should lie; neither the son of man that HE should repent: hath HE said, and shall HE not do it? Or hath HE spoken, and shall HE not make it good?

Numbers 23:19

2 In hope of eternal life, which God, that cannot lie, promised before the world began.

Titus 1: 2

There is one truth of God's Word that we need to hold on to today. When God makes a promise, HE means it. When HE says something; it is a rock that you can build your life on. HE cannot lie !! When the Word of God says that Jesus loves me, HE proved it by dying on the cross for my sins. John 15: 13 says Greater love have no man than this, that a man lay down his life for his friends. Jesus proved HIS love by the actions that HE demonstrated. HE just can't lie! It is not in HIS nature. Satan is the father of lies (John 8:44). He will either tell you a lie, or even worse…a half truth. Remember what he told eve in the garden. He told her you shall not surely die. Eve did not physically die right then, but she eventually did. Adam and Eve did experience a spiritual death, and no longer had the close intimate relationship with God, that they had enjoyed before their sin. Satan told them a partial truth, with just enough deception, to lead them to eventual destruction.

When you are going through the tough battles of life, think about the promises of God. HE said that I will never leave you, nor forsake you (Hebrews 13:5). Many of us have been in terrible Job-like trials. We have seen those closest to us turn on us. We have had issues on our jobs. We have cried in the midnight hour, and who shows up…Jesus ! HE said HE would never leave us or forsake us, and that is a promise, and HE cannot lie ! Jesus told HIS disciples that HE was going to the cross to die for our sins, and rise on the third day. On the third day; Jesus rose from the dead...JUST LIKE HE PROMISED AND HE CANNOT LIE.

Today...take God at HIS word. Remember HE will do what HE promised. Trust HIM today, and receive your victory...God Bless.

SEVENTY-SIX

12 Beloved, think it not strange concerning the firey trial which is try you as though some strange thing happened unto you, as though some strange thing happened unto you:

13 But rejoice, in as much as ye are partakers of Christ's sufferings: that, when HIS glory shall be revealed, ye may be glad with exceeding joy.

In 2nd Corinthians 4:8, the Apostle Paul wrote, We are troubled on every side, yet not destressed. Whether it was the Apostle Paul, or Simon Peter, or any of us, we have the same life status in common. We all go through trials, and many of those trials can be extremely tough. 1st Peter 4: 12 reads, "Beloved, think it not strange concerning the firey trial, which try you. We often dwell on the fire of the trial, instead of the word "Beloved". The word beloved literally means that we are deeply loved. Jesus Christ truly loves us with AGAPE love. AGAPE is one of the Greek words for love. This is the true love of Christ. Not the word Philia or "Friendship". By the way, most of the love we have is based on feeling. The love of Jesus Christ is a deep, abiding, self-sacrificing love. That is how Jesus loves us. Psalm 119:75, the Psalmist wrote I know, O Lord that thy judgements are right, and that thou if faithfulness hast afflicted me. **You see, when we are in the firey trial, THAT IS GOD DEMONSTRATING HIS LOVE FOR US. HIS true AGAPE love, cannot leave us as a spiritual infant. Jesus faithfulness and love for us, is demonstrated by sometimes allowing us to go through. The firey trial is actually necessary. The Apostle Paul was troubled on every side, but also wrote in Romans 8, that he is more than a conqueror in Christ Jesus.

I am pleading with a reader of this devotional today, not to quit on Jesus, stay in the fight. You will find that the AGAPE love of Jesus, will become so very real to you in the trial. How you carry yourself in the trial, will bring hope to someone else, who is truly in the fight of THEIR life. Verse 13 says rejoice in the midst of the trial. Give Jesus praise and glory in the trial. Do not wait until the victory is won, know that Jesus loves you, and allowed the trial, and rejoice now. Jesus loves you and I, and wants the glory though your firey trial.

Marriage is a beautiful creation, and is a picture of Christ and the church (Ephesians 5). Marriage is also one of the most common places, where the firey trial takes place. It is through some of my marital trials, that my faith in Jesus grew, and I learned how important it is to forgive, and ask forgiveness for my mistakes. During some of deep and painful trials in my own family, has allowed me to help or encourage someone else, who is in their firey trial. When your body is ailing, and racked with pain, and you experience to loving comfort and healing of Jesus, you can minister to someone during their sickness.

Today...know that the firey trial in your life works for your good (Romans 8:28). Remember, Jesus loves you very much, and the firey trial is not strange. Jesus wants to get HIS glory in your trial. Hold on to HIM today...God Bless.

SEVENTY-SEVEN

3 Now the man Moses was very meek, above all the men which were upon the face of the earth.

Numbers 12:3

11 But the meek shall inherit the earth, and shall delight themselves in the abundance of peace.

Psalm 37:11

5 Blessed are the meek, for they shall inherit the earth.

Matthew 5: 5

22 But the fruit of the Spirit is love (AGAPE), joy, peace, longsuffering, gentleness, goodness, faith,

23 Meekness, temperance, against such there is no law.

Galatians 5: 22-23

Do you want to be the strongest, mightiest man or woman today? Do you truly want to walk in the power an anointing of God? Do you want to see victory come in the most difficult of circumstances? Look at these Old and New Testament scriptures. Moses was a meek man, above all other men. His confidence was completely in the Lord. In Psalm 37, David wrote in Psalm 37:11, the meek shall inherit the earth. Jesus said in the Sermon on the Mount...Blessed are the meek for they shall inherit the earth.

The Apostle Paul was a proud Jewish Pharisee, when he was Saul of Tarsus. He persecuted the Church of Jesus without mercy. He dragged men and women to prison, and had no mercy. In Acts Chapter 7, Paul (Saul at that time), stood in agreement with the men who stoned Stephen. He held their garments, while they carried out the stoning. All Stephen did was preach Jesus! Stephen forgave the men who stoned him with his dying breath.

Saul of Tarsus never forgot the meekness, mercy and love demonstrated by Stephen. In Acts Chapter 9, Saul was on his way to Damascus to imprison and kill more Christians. Jesus knocked him off his donkey (and his high horse). Jesus said. "Saul, Saul, why do you persecute me"? ** We see nowhere in scripture where Saul ever persecuted Jesus personally. Jesus said in Matthew 25, Whatsoever ye do to the least of these my brethren, ye have done it unto me. ** This should bring us to more meekness and humility, and truly make us consider how we treat on another.

After Jesus blinds Saul of Tarsus for 3 days in Acts 9, he was humbled, and repentive. He went into Damascus, and Ananias came to him, and baptized him. Saul of Tarsus was now a new creature in Christ Jesus, and was then filled with the Holy Ghost. He became the Apostle Paul. As Paul ministered to the churches, it is amazing how this proud man was converted, and like Moses taught, like David taught, and like Jesus taught, meekness is now taught as a fruit of the spirit of God.

The work of God is done by humble men and women, who move in greater and greater anointing, as they move in a spirit of meekness. John the Baptist said in John 3: 30…He (Jesus) must increase, I must decrease. When you are lowly, and meek before God, all the power of Heaven is with you. **Meekness is a true fruit of the Spirit. Meekness in us, is a clear that Jesus is in us, and pride is moving out of us.

Today…let us all walk in a spirit of meekness, taking a humble road toward God and one another. Jesus will have HIS way, and bring victory into our lives…God Bless.

$\mathcal{S}$EVENTY-EIGHT

6 Blessed are they which do hunger and thirst after righteousness,
for they shall be filled.

Matthew 5:6

What are you truly hungry for today? Jesus said Blessed are they which do hunger and thirst after righteousness, for they shall be filled. Proverbs 27:7 says that the full soul loves the honeycomb, but to the hungry soul, every bitter thing is sweet. If I am full of this modern culture, and its hatred, and division, and bitterness, you will never get full of what you need. We need to be full of Jesus, and HIS Word, and HIS ways. When we fill ourselves with all the world has to offer, and all of the things that the devil sends with that, we will not desire the good things of God. We will not have peace in the midst of a storm. Look at the people around you, who continually complain about life. They are FULL of all the world's misery. Jesus gave us a key to overcome all of this. He said to hunger and thirst after righteousness, and you shall be filled.

This world today has so many pitfalls, and snares. The world has never had more depression and oppression. Jesus said to hunger and thirst after HIS righteousness. Spouses are leaving marriages, and saying that they no longer love their mate. How can this be, when 1st Corinthians 13 says love (AGAPE) endures all things. What are you hungering and thirsty for? If I hunger and thirst after righteousness, I can do life the way Jesus wants it done. When I can do that, I can see the miracles that Jesus wants me have.

The Word of God in the 37th Psalm tells us to delight ourselves in the Lord, and HE will give us the desires of our hearts. Notice that David wrote that before you receive the desires of your heart, you must first DELIGHT YOURSELF IN THE LORD. Your heavenly blessings come WHEN YOU HUNGER AND THIRST AFTER RIGHTEUSNESS.

A great way to illustrate Jesus' word here is to picture a thirsty man crawling across the desert. He is desperate for just a small drink, just to sustain himself, and stay alive. It is over 100 degrees in extreme humidity. That is how to think of the level of hunger and thirst that one needs, in seeking out the righteousness of Christ. ** THAT IS HOW I CAN LOVE AND FORGIVE THROUGH HURT, PAIN, AND REJECTION. I hunger and thirst after the way that Jesus responds. I get a Christ-like victory, because I hunger and thirst after Christ-like responses.

Today... become a truly blessed man or woman. The key is to hunger and thirst after the righteousness of Christ...God Bless.

SEVENTY-NINE

20 If a man say, I love God, and hate his brother, he is a liar: for he that loves not his brother whom he hath seen, how can he love God, whom he hath not seen?

1st John 4: 20

11 Beloved, if God so loved us, we ought to love one another.

1st John 4: 11

WE ARE NOT LIARS !! We do love one another. At least, we should check ourselves today, and make sure that we are walking in this Word. ** We say that we want to make it to heaven, and to spend eternity with Jesus. We must however know how much weight that Jesus puts on us not being liars, and having true love one for another. Consider what Revelation 21:27 says on the subject…And there shall in no wise enter into it anything that defileth, neither whatsoever worketh abomination, OR MAKETH A LIE: but they which are written in the Lambs Book of Life.

1st John 4: 19 says…We loved HIM, because HE first loved us. I do not deserve the love of Jesus (none of us do). Romans 3:10 says…As it is written, there is none righteous; no not one. Maybe you sought out salvation in Jesus at a young age, and were always sensitive to HIS Word. I was not so fortunate, and rejected the love of Christ until I was nearly 31 years old. I could speak a few religious clichés, and go to church on occasion. Once at a Communion service in the church that I grew up in, I had an experience with God. The pastor did something out of the ordinary at the early service. He had all of us come to the front of the church in the pulpit area, and join hands in a circle, and pray at Communion time. There was only 12 or 14 of us there at the time. As we prayed, I truly felt something literally shoot through me. This was very unfamiliar to me. I was only about 16 or 17 at the time, and was living very sinfully. Little did I know that this was a true touch from Jesus. HE was lovingly drawing me to HIMSELF, and this was such a warm and loving presence. This was an experience that felt 20 times greater that all of the sin that I was committing. Jesus showed me that HE loved me long before I ever thought to serve HIM faithfully.

Since Jesus went to great lengths to draw me to HIMSELF, how could I not share HIS loving message with everyone I meet? HOW THEN COULD I NOT LOVE AND FORGIVE MY BROTHERS? I AM NOT A LIAR!!

I have not seen God, however I read of HIS awesome love in HIS Word. When we read how much HE loves us, I MUST love the brother or sister that I see. I absolutely must show the Agape love of Jesus to them, or be declared a LIAR. I AM NOT A LIAR...I DO LOVE THE BRETHREN.

This AGAPE love in UNCONDITIONAL. It does not shift or change with my emotions. 1st Corinthians is the LOVE chapter. Notice how verse 7 says that love (AGAPE not Philia) bears all things, believes all things, hopes all things, ENDURES ALL THINGS. Love is able to remain and grow through the deepest hurts and pains. Love can remain through betrayal. How you ask?? Remember the cross, and how Jesus truly, truly loved you first. When you think on Jesus on the cross, HIS loving sacrifice, HIS loving kindness, and merciful forgiveness toward us, it becomes much easier to love one another.

Today...make it clear to God and man that you are not a liar. Show how you appreciate the love and forgiveness of Christ, by loving and forgiving Everyone today and always...God Bless.

ℰIGHTY

*1 All the commandments which I command thee this day shall ye
observe to do, that ye may live, and multiply, and go in and possess
the land which the Lord sware unto your fathers.*

*2 And thou shalt remember all the way which the Lord thy God
led thee these forty years in the wilderness, to humble thee, and
to prove thee, to know what was in thine heart, whether thou
wouldest keep his commandments or no.*

*3 And He humbled thee, and suffered thee to hunger, and fed thee
with manna, which thou knewest not, neither did thy fathers
know; that He might make thee to know that man doth not live
by bread only, but by every word that proceedeth out of the mouth
of God.*

Deuteronomy 8:1-3

This may explain some of the MAJOR trials in our lives. You have a mountain in front of you, and you have been praying, and praying. This mountain does not seem to be moving; or the situation is getting worse. You have prayed and even spent time in fasting (friends, I have been here). You read Mark 11: 20-24, and you are confident that you can make the mountain move by faith. You are confident that the situation will change and victory will come. Yet, delay after delay after delay takes place through your prayer and intercession. Look at these verses in Deuteronomy, and DO NOT QUIT IN THE WAITING. The children of Israel were wandering in the desert, and waiting and waiting to enter into the promised land. God was watching, and checking out what was inside of the people. HE suffered, or made them to wander, basically in circles for 40 years. No, before you believe that the wait for your blessing is going to be 40 years, understand that a multitude was being led through the wilderness, after 400 years of bondage in Egypt. God got Israel out of Egypt, but HE had to get the Egypt ways out of Israel.

Consider, what verse 2 says. The Lord was humbling Israel, and checking what was in their heart. HE had to do that, considering the magnitude of victory that HE was going to bring them. The power of God was going to make nation after nation fall in front of the armies of Israel. HE was bringing the Jewish people into an understanding of HIS ways.

Now, consider what YOU are asking for. You are asking Jesus to recover a spouse, save a child, heal someone, provide a financial miracle, or just deliver you. You may be bound by alcohol, drugs, hatred, racism, bitterness, or pornography. You and I want to get delivered from ANYTHING that would keep us out of Glory. You are about to see the mountain (or mountains) move. **When Jesus does this, WILL YOU GIVE HIM THE GLORY? Will you be faithful in church, after a loving God blesses you in a mighty way? You prayed, and asked help from the Lord, to get you a car, because you need to get to work. HE blesses you with a better vehicle than you imagined, and a raise on your job to make sure you can afford it. **Now after the blessing, you stay home on Sunday, and skip church. Now, you have to wash the car on Sunday. This is why we sometimes have to wait, and go through unpleasant experiences. Israel had to wander, and suffer hunger and thirst. The murmuring and complaining was revealed in the wandering. The Lord did however provide for them in the waiting, as HE will do for us. HE loves us so much that HE wants us to be blessed, but to worship the BLESSER; not the BLESSING!!.

Idolatry and unfaithfulness are not a joke to Jesus. If you are praying for your children, you cannot compromise, or leave Jesus for them. (Jesus said in Matthew 10:37...whoever loves father or mother, or son or daughter more than Jesus is not worthy of HIM...Those are HIS Words). HE wants to answer you with HIS power and might, and bring you great blessing. Jesus, however will check you first to see what is inside.

Today...Remember the waiting is part of the process. Surrender all of you to Jesus, and while HE is getting the Egypt out of you and me; know that if we continue with HIM; the promised land is coming...God Bless.

$\mathcal{E}$IGHTY-ONE

1 Blessed is the man that walketh not in the counsel of the ungodly, nor standeth in the way of sinners, nor sitteth in the seat of the scornful.

2 But his delight is in the law of the Lord, and in his law doth he meditate day and night.

3 And he shall be like a tree planted by the rivers of water, that bringeth forth his fruit in his season; his leaf also shall not wither; and whatsoever he doeth shall prosper.

Psalms 1 :1-3

In times like these, what I listen to matters. Remember the words of the great American Patriot Thomas Paine...These are the times that try men's souls. The Apostle Paul called these end time events as "Perilous Times", in 2nd Timothy 3. To keep my mind stable and grounded, to walk in blessings and victory... REJECT EVIL COMMUNICATION!! Psalm 1 says...Blessed is the man who walks NOT in the counsel of the ungodly, nor stands in the way of sinners, nor sits in the seat of the scornful. Verse 2 says that the blessed person meditates on the Word of the Lord... DAY AND NIGHT. Why does listening to the Word matter? Why does rejecting the defeating word of evil communication matter? Proverbs 16:25 says...There is a way that SEEMS right to a man, the end thereof are the ways of death. The events of the day are challenging, if not just plain frightening. What we keep our mind on truly matters. I spoke at a school several years ago. They were in mourning, because a very popular student had recently died. She had never used drugs or alcohol ever. Someone talked her into using ecstasy one time. She had a reaction and died. She had been the president of the school SADD Chapter. One time yielding to evil communication does matter. Psalm 1:3 reminds us that prosperity and victory comes by hearkening to the Word of God. You are likened to healthy tree bringing forth fruit. The choice is yours.

Today... Choose the life, blessings, and victory in God's Word, and reject the evil communication that leads to defeat and destruction... God bless.

$\mathcal{E}$IGHTY-TWO

3 I thou Lord, shouldst mark iniquities, O Lord, who shall stand?

4 But there is forgiveness with thee, that thou mayest be feared.
Psalm 130: 3-4

18 If he hath wronged thee, or if he oweth thee ought, put that on
my account.
Philemon 1: 18

If Jesus marked every iniquity that we committed, and gave us no remedy for redemption…WE WOULD BE WORSE THAN DOOMED!! It is so easy to see why Jesus said in Mark 7, that what defiles us is not what goes into us; not what we eat, but the thoughts of the heart, that come out of us. If Jesus marked iniquity, where would we be? Where would we be if Jesus sent HIS ultimate judgement on us for every evil thought or word? Who would stand if the Lord marked iniquity? I have observed incredibly cruel, and undeniably evil thoughts and words from people in church, and out of church. I have observed deep hateful iniquity, horrible words of dark bitterness come out of people, who name the name of Jesus. They claim to be Christian, which means "Christ-like". If Jesus marked iniquity, who would stand? The answer is no one would stand. Romans 3:10 is so sobering…As it is written; there is none righteous; no not one.

Please let me be clear; I am not the Prodigal son's older brother, who was truly lost in "self" righteousness. I know that I stand guilty for my own dose of evil thoughts and iniquity. I have felt the internal pain, when battling to forgive. I have felt the weakness of fleshly lust, and the guilt that follows. After having those thoughts, I have then had to go out and preach righteousness to others, knowing my imperfections. I need the mercy of Jesus. That is why I love the short one chapter Book of Philemon. The Apostle Paul was a man of spiritual authority in Philemon's life. A man named Onesimus, was a servant and bondman to Philemon. He committed what was a horrible offense in that culture, and ran away from Philemon. While he was fleeing from Philemon met the Apostle Paul, who did what Paul always did so faithfully (we should too); he preached Jesus to Onesimus. He was born again in Jesus at the preaching of Paul. Paul sent the letter to Philemon, and told him to forgive Onesimus completely. Not only did Philemon forgive this man, but Onesimus would later become his pastor. You cannot have a bitter heart of unforgiveness and iniquity, and have a glorious testimony like this. For Jesus to get the glory in your life, and do great things, there must be forgiveness, like Psalm 130: 4 says…But there is forgiveness with thee, that thou mayest be feared.

Philemon forgave Onesimus; Jesus got the glory. One of the ways that came to pass was Stephen, forgiving the Saul of Tarsus, when he was stoned. Saul became the Apostle Paul, who would later preach to Onesimus. Jesus forgave Simon Peter for denying him. Peter went on to be used to open the church in Acts 2 for the Jews, and Acts 10 for the Gentiles.

The choice always falls back on us. Do we live like Jesus has no knowledge of our iniquity? None of us would stand if Jesus marks our iniquity. READ REVELATION 20: 10-15…THERE ARE BOOKS OF REMEMBRANCE. The is also a Book of Life; where the names of those redeemed in Jesus, who repent, and forgive, and truly cry out to Jesus with an earnest heart. These don't take the Mercy of God for granted. They remember the iniquity that Jesus forgave them for…THEY COMPLETELY FORGIVE EVERYBODY FOR EVERYTHING.

Today…remember that if Jesus would mark or forever hold our iniquity against us; we would be finished. Examine your heart today; forgive everyone; for everything…God Bless.

EIGHTY-THREE

12 For ye shall not go out with haste, nor go by flight: for the Lord will go before you; and the God of Israel will be your rereward (rear guard).

Isaiah 52:12

1 Lord, how are they incensed that trouble me! Many there be that rise up against me.

2 Many there be which say of my soul, there is no help for him in God. Selah.

3 But thou, O Lord, art a shield for me: my glory and the lifter of mine head.

Who is going through a battle today? Does the situation appear too tough? When King David wrote Psalm 3, he was going through the toughest battle in his life. You think that Goliath was the toughest battle of his life, but in Psalm 3, he was facing something taller that Goliath. You have certainly had to face this Goliath too. The giant in Psalm 3 that David was facing was betrayal. He was being pursued by his own son Absalom. It was not as though David had never done wrong, he had. It is not like we have not done wrong in our lives...We All Have! Never forget Romans 3:23, For all have sinned, and come short of the glory of God.

Whether David was wrong or not in his life, he was very troubled. His son Absalom turned on him, and became his bitter enemy. Imagine your own son turning on you, stealing the heart of the people, and then stealing the kingdom. David, literally had to flee for his life. He was being pursued by people, who once looked to him as their king. Keep in mind that Jesus was betrayed by one of his disciples. Zechariah 13: 6 says...And one shall say unto him: What are these wounds in in thine hands? Then he shall answer; those with which I wounded in the house of my friends. Psalm 41: 9 and John 13:18 both describe the betrayal by Judas. It reads...My own familiar friend has lifted up his heel against me.

Isaiah 52: 12 tells us that the God of Israel shall go before you, and also be your rearguard...He's got your back. David understood that the Lord is a shield, and would lift up his head. Psalm 34:7 says that the Lord camps HIS angels round about them that fear HIM, and delivers them. HE is a shield, and truly defended David against the betrayal of his son. Absalom was defeated, and David was returned to the throne. God was truly David's defender. To show God's heart was David's heart, even after Absalom betrayed David, David was still concerned about Absalom. Romans 12 tells us to love them that hate you, and pray for those, who despitefully use you. That is the real victory over hurtful betrayal.

Today...Know that Jesus has your back, and will fight for you, even in the most hurtful betrayal. Your weapon is just as important: forgive and pray for the betrayer...God Bless.

ℰIGHTY-FOUR

5 It is better to hear the rebuke of the wise, than for a man to hear the song of fools.

Ecclesiastes 8:5

5 Open rebuke is better than secret love.

6 Faithful are the wounds of a friend: but the kisses of an enemy are deceitful

Proverbs 27:5-6

16 Am I therefore become your enemy, because I tell you the truth?

Galatians 4:16

When a brother or sister tells you what you NEED to hear, do you get angry? In Galatians 4:16, the Apostle Paul asks a question…Am I therefore become your enemy, because I tell you the truth? If you are going down a road that will take you away from Jesus, is it good that I let you fall off the cliff of disaster, or should I warn you? In 1992, my then 92-year-old grandmother told me that if I did not get saved, and surrender my life to Jesus, I had a problem coming directly into a part of my life. Was she my enemy for telling me the truth? The very thing that she warned me about (BY THE WAY…I IGNORED HER LOVING WORDS OF WARNING) came to pass, just like she said. I could have avoided a lot of heart ache, and pain by simply taking heed to what a very godly woman, who was 92 years young had to say. 1st Timothy 2:4 says that is God's will for all men to be saved, and come to the knowledge of the truth. Truly, I should have listened…my grandmother was giving the faithful words of a friend…TRULY SHE WAS NOT AN ENEMY!!

The Word of God reminds us that open rebuke is better that secret love. Faithful are the wounds of a friend, but the kisses of an enemy are deceitful. Proverbs 17: 17 says, A friend loveth at all times, and a brother is born for adversity. King Solomon penned Proverbs, and the Book of Ecclesiastes. He was much older when he wrote Ecclesiastes. He had many failures in his life, and times where the wisest man who had ever lived (until Jesus came), should have followed the counsel of his father David. David warned Solomon, and all who would hear, to avoid idolatry, and never worship another god. When you read 1 Kings 11th Chapter, you can see how Solomon lost his way. We can lose our way, simply by turning a deaf ear to good advice. A friend loves at all times (even when we are not loving, or easily loved) and should be willing to give a good word of warning when needed. We should be a good friend, and be willing to hear a good word of warning. ** King Rehoboam was Solomon's son. After Solomon died, he became king. The old wise men gave him good advice. The younger men of his age, gave bad advice, that ended up dividing the whole nation of Israel.

A wise man will hear. Pride and stubbornness keep our ears dull to what words really help us in a time of need. I have had some very hurtful things leveled at me. When I have sought counsel, from the few that I trust in that role, I notice that those in my camp, always tell me to love, forgive, and stay close to Jesus, and HIS Word. When someone comes to me, and says that they have been betrayed by a spouse, or child, or co-worker, is it any wonder that I always advise them to love, and forgive, and stay close to Jesus.

Today…remember that a true friend, will give you the Word of God in a time of need. A true friend will tell us what we need to hear, not just what we want to hear. A wise man or woman will take that good word to heart, and move according to the Word of God, and have victory…God Bless.

&IGHTY-FIVE

7a For they have sown the wind; they shall reap the whirlwind…

Hosea 8:7a

7 Be not deceived: God is not mocked: for whatsoever a man soweth, that shall he also reap.

8 For he that soweth to his flesh, shall of the flesh reap corruption; but he that soweth to the spirit, shall of the spirit real life everlasting.

9: And let us be not weary in well doing: for in due season we shall reap, if we faint not.

Galatians 6: 7-9

How we treat others MATTERS !! I have apologized again and again, and sometimes for things, that the person I apologize to, has no idea what I am talking about. This comes from the pure, pure conviction that Jesus sends us. In 1st and 2nd Corinthians, the scripture reads…LET A MAN EXAMINE HIMSELF. After I do, I seem to always find an area of my life to repent about. I sincerely want to treat others, as I want to be treated (The Golden Rule of Matthew 7:12). There are times when I have not treated others as well I should. I have seen that if I sow a humble, repentive state, I seem to receive an extreme amount of mercy, when I am terribly wrong. Jesus is such a fair and equitable God. He left the scripture in Galatians 7: 9, to remind us that we should never be weary or tired in well doing; for HE will not forget our good works.

On the other hand, when we sow evil, we will beget or birth evil. We should read the scripture in Hosea 8 verse 7, and consider. They have sown the wind, they shall reap the whirlwind. Sometimes people do not consider the evil that they do, because of God's mercy. They attack others, and nothing happens right away. They sow to the wind, and attack their brother or sister. They never think that the whirlwind is coming. Israel was called the "Apple of God's eye" in Zechariah 2:8. Look at history, and it is easy to see how much God despises those who attack Israel, and the Jewish people. The list is long of those who sowed to the wind: Sennacharib in the old days; Hitler and Stalin and Gamel Naser in modern times. All faced judgement for their evil against the Apple of God's eye.

In the new Testament, Jesus makes it clear...WHATSOEVER WE DO TO THE LEAST OF THESE MY BROTHERS, YOU HAVE DONE IT UNTO ME. Please read Acts Chapter 9, and see where Saul of Tarsus viciously attacked and persecuted the church. He was on the way to Damascus to arrest, imprison, and kill more Christians. When Jesus knocked him off of his donkey, and blinded him, HIS words to Saul were amazing. Jesus said...Saul, Saul, why do you persecute ME. Jesus meant what HE said in Matthew 25...WHAT YOU DO TO YOUR BROTHER OR SISTER, YOU HAVE DONE UNTO JESUS. That is a two way street, so if I bless Jesus, by blessing and doing well to my brother or sister, I am bringing that blessing back to my own doorstep.

Today...Let us consider how we treat one another. Let us sow the good and reap the good, and watch the blessing manifest in our lives...God Bless.

ℰIGHTY-SIX

7 Wherefore as the Holy Ghost saith, Today if ye will hear his voice,

8 Harden not your hearts, as in the provocation, in the day of temptation in the wilderness:

9 When your fathers tempted me, proved me, and saw my works forty years.

10 Wherefore I was grieved with that generation, and said, They do always err in their heart; and they have not known my ways.

11 So I sware in my wrath, They shall not enter into my rest.

Hebrews 3: 7-11

Why prolong the situation, when you don't have to? Why make the bad last longer and longer in duration? That is kind of like being in the ring, with the hardest puncher in the world, and hanging on to the ropes, so that he can keep on punching you in the corner. He steps back to let you out of the corner. You cling to the ropes, and say, "No ! I am going to stay in this corner, and let you hit me". ** This is what it is like when you and I harden our hearts, and miss out on a deliverance from a tough situation. We serve a God, who absolutely loves to bring us out of difficult, and even impossible situations. Israel, the "Apple of God's Eye", was continually in the most challenging circumstances. After 400 years of bondage in Egypt, God brought Israel out, with the help and hand of Moses. HE set them up for total victory, and led them TO the Red Sea. God set the Children of Israel up, to make a 40-day journey. The Red Sea would be parted, Egypt defeated, and a quick trip to the promised land assured.

Hebrews 3rd and 4th Chapters explain how a 40-day journey, turned into a 40 year ordeal, that left a generation, to die off in the desert. **They (like We do sometimes) hardened their heart. We allow pride to enter in, and miss out on God's breakthrough. We argue with the pastor, or the minister, or the pastor's wife, and must hold on to our position and opinion. ** I raise this question to you today. Is winning the argument more important than the deliverance from the situation?

Moses brought the word of God to the people, who continually contended with him. They became very hard hearted. They became extremely stubborn, and were even called "stiff-necked". Before we are too hard on Israel, let's consider how many times WE are stubborn and down right hard hearted. Not all the Children of Israel were hard hearted. There were some with the humble, obedient, faithful, and loyal mind, of a Joshua and Caleb. They did not join in with stubbornness, pride, or a hard-hearted character. They were the only two, who did not die in the wilderness. Joshua and Caleb received their inheritance, when all their generation tempted god in the wilderness. Their generation did not believe, when the Word of God was preached. Joshua and Caleb, rejected evil reports, evil communication, false and rebellious words, and a hard-hearted character. They waited 40 years too, however they did receive the promise. The promise delayed, was not a promise denied.

I had a situation on my job many years ago. I had some very difficult days with a coworker. Truly, I focused on the coworker, and developed a hard and unforgiving heart. The situation lasted for two and a half years. I finally listened to Jesus, who revealed to me that the problem was ME. Jesus was removing pride, and rebellion from my heart. When I submitted to HIS Word, the situation moved. Like Israel, I prolonged my own walk through the wilderness.

Today...take a look at the condition of your heart. Is it the Joshua and Caleb heart, that receives the blessings, or is it the heart that is hard, stubborn, and full of pride? Are making your 40-day journey, or prolonging it to 40 years? The choice is yours...God Bless.

$\mathcal{E}$IGHTY-SEVEN

*12 For the eyes of the Lord are over the righteous, and HIS ears are open unto their prayers: **but the face of the Lord is against them that do evil.***

1st Peter 3:12

3 The eyes of the Lord are in every place, beholding the evil and the good.

Proverbs 15:3

Jesus is watching today. I want HIM to be pleased with what HE sees. I want HIM to keep HIS eyes on me. When I pray, I want Jesus to hear me. When I go from place to place, I want HIM to camp HIS angels around me. Did you know that Psalm 34: 7 says that the Lord camps HIS angels round about them that fear HIM, and delivers them? Contrast that to John 9:31, which says... Now we know that God heareth not sinners; but if any man be a worshipper of God, and doeth HIS will, him HE heareth. So, Jesus puts HIS eyes on those who are redeemed by the Name of Jesus, and washed in the Blood of Jesus. What an amazing truth !!

HE also makes it clear, that if I want to live a sinful life, I too will have the eyes of the Lord on me. The result however, in the end is different. I Jeremiah 29: 11...The word of God says...For I know the thoughts that I think toward you saith the Lord, thoughts of peace, and not of evil, to give you an expected end. What an excellent promise. When you look at Jeremiah 44:11, the same God says HIS face is against Israel. Why was there such a change, because the actions of the people, was to clearly rebel against God's Word. The eyes of the Lord were upon them too.

This is my heart's cry today...Lord Jesus...Keep your eyes on me. Do not let me wander away from you. When I am hurt of betrayed...let me forgive.

When evil comes my way…Let me respond with love. Why? Because I want the Eyes of the Lord to stay upon me. I want HIS ears open to my prayers.

Today…Live so that the Eyes of the Lord are upon you for good. Live so that HIS ears are open unto your prayers…God Bless.

&IGHTY-EIGHT

8 Be sober, be vigilant, because your adversary the devil, as a roaring lion, walketh about seeking whom he may he may devour.

9 Whom resist steadfast in the faith, knowing that the same afflictions are accomplished in your brethren that are in the world.

This is the thought for the day. Are you really angry at your brother or sister? Is the thing that they did a mole hill, and you are turning it into a mountain. The is a devil, who the Word of God in 1ˢᵗ Peter likens to a lion, looking for a vulnerable piece of meat; someone to devour. He can devour any one of us, who let his voice into our ears. When satan gats the opportunity, he magnifies every situation, and makes you doubt your brother or sister.

Think about the writer of this book…Simon Peter. He was a man chosen by Jesus; like a lot of us. He was inexperienced in spiritual things; like a lot of us. He was quick to speak ahead of his own experiences, and proclaim what he would do; like a lot of us. Yet, with all of Peter's imperfections, he was the one chosen to open the church for Jews (Acts 2) and the Gentiles (Acts 10). HE WAS ALSO THE MAN WHO DENIED JESUS 3 TIMES, AND CURSED OUT A LITTLE GIRL, WHO INSISTED THAT HE WAS A DISCIPLE OF JESUS!!. In Galatians 2, Paul corrected Peter for his spiritual bigotry toward the Gentiles. He literally created confusion in the Church of Jesus Christ, between the Jewish and Gentile believers.

I mentioned some the things that Peter failed in, to illustrate that he was a man, who had been tripped up by the devil many times. Satan attempted to destroy his ministry. John 10:10 is true, the devil is a thief, and comes to steal, kill, and destroy. He WILL destroy anything you give him access to. Peter of ALL people knew that best. He also knew that he and Judas both let Jesus down. One betrayed him to the Pharisees, but the other denied HIM when it counted. Judas was tricked into suicide by the devil…PETER KNEW

ABOUT SATAN'S MENTAL AND SPIRITUAL ATTACK, THAT LED TO JUDAS' SUICIDE.

Since Peter was a Man of God, who understood the devil's mental games, he; led of the Spirit, wrote this clear warning to us. Resist him steadfast, by faith, in faith, and with the knowledge that Peter was imparting to us. Verse 9 says that the same afflictions are being suffered by all of our brothers in the world. We are all going through one fight or another, against the one who "like" a roaring lion, is going to attempt to devour us.

Today…be aware!! Take Peter's warning to heart. Know that satan is looking for an inch, so that he can take 10 miles out of your life. Be sober, be vigilant… watch out for satan's attempts to steal your mind, your peace, your family, and finally your salvation…God Bless.

EIGHTY-NINE

9 But ye are a chosen generation, a royal priesthood, a holy nation, an holy nation, a peculiar people, that ye should show forth the praises of him, who hath called you out of darkness, into his marvelous light.

10 Which in time past were not a people, but are now the people of God: which had not obtained mercy, but now have obtained mercy.

Please change your mind today. You may have gotten out of bed the way I have had to some days. Yes, I am writing this, and am admitting to all of you reading this, that some days I am going through between the ears. You need to know that 1st Peter 4: 12 is correct. This is not a strange thing to experience. When your family situation is NOT what you expected, or your marriage, or your finances, or your health, you can easily think the wrong things. You can think that the problems in your life are ALL about you, and if you were really anything special, you would not be going through betrayal, despair, and major life frustration.

Please remember Job, David, Jonathan, Zechariah, and many others in the Old Testament, and all the things that they went through. Then, thing about Peter, crucified upside down, Paul, shipwrecked, beaten, and later beheaded. How about John, boiled in oil, and exiled to the Isle of Patmos. If all of these men were not supposed to suffer anything because they were chosen of God, then why did they go through these things. In 2nd Corinthians 12...the Apostle Paul wrote that, HIS grace is sufficient (enough to sustain us), and is made perfect in weakness. Through all of HIS suffering, Paul knew that he was part of the Royal Priesthood. He knew when in Acts 9, Jesus knocked him off donkey, and blinded him, it was part of Jesus choosing him, and making him great in HIS kingdom. Paul seemed to always know who he was, no matter what. WE NEED TO KNOW THAT TOO.

You may be having a day when you do not think of yourself as less than Child of God (All of us have been here) and you believe that the horrible issues of your life dictate who you are, remember these verses in 1st Peter. When born again in Jesus, you become a Royal Priesthood (According to Psalm 4:3...we are set apart so that God hears our prayers), an Holy Nation (A people set apart to be different in this world), a peculiar people (precious and purchased by the Blood of Jesus), and of course a Chosen Generation (personally selected by Jesus for HIS purpose).

Jesus promised to hear you, even if your spouse or children will not. Jesus promised to NEVER leave you of forsake you in Hebrews 13:5 (New Testament), even if your spouse or children do leave you. It becomes very important to let the Word of God define you, and not other people. It important to look at the mirror of the Word of God, and not the piece of glass in front of you. YOU ARE SPECIAL WHETHER YOU THINK YOU ARE OR NOT...GET RID OF DEPRESSION, NEGATIVE, AND DEFEATING THOUGHTS. **NEVER THINK OF SUICIDE...YOU ARE THAT PRECIOUS ROYAL PRIESTHOOD. DO NOT HOLD ON TO OFFENSES...FORGIVE...YOU ARE THE CHOSEN VESSEL TO HEAR JESUS' VOICE, AND FOR HIM TO HEAR YOUR PRAYERS.

Today...remember who you are. Meditate today on 1st Peter 2:9-10, and know that you are chosen by the KING OF KINGS to be royalty in this world... God bless.

$\mathcal{N}$INETY

8 If you fulfill the royal law according to the scripture, Thou shalt love thy neighbor as thyself, ye shall do well.

9 But if ye have respect of persons, ye commit sin and are convinced of the law as transgressors.

When we fulfill the love of Christ, there is a right way and a wrong way. Jesus said in John 15:12; This new commandment I give you, that ye love one another, as I have loved you. Romans 13: 8 says to Owe no man anything, but to love one another; for he that loveth another has fulfilled the law. I am challenging you and me today. We love to use the word "Love". Many of you grew up, or are faithfully attending a ministry. You may know that the New testament was written in Greek, and translated to English. We then have several different Greek words for love, and they are not all the same, and have much different strength.

Agape is the self-sacrificing, unconditional love of Christ. It is not the kind of Philia or Brotherly Love that has conditions. 2nd Peter 1st Chapter says that you have to add to Brotherly Love. It is not complete, you have to add to it, so that you will not be a respecter of persons. A respecter of persons does not treat people the same, NO MATTER WHAT. The Word of God calls this sin. If I forgive a friend, especially one who is not in the household of faith, and will not forgive a brother in Christ; you then sin, and the name of that sin is "Respecter of Persons". I forgive this one, and not that one. I will love this one, but not that one…That's a respecter of persons. Love is love, and is not conditional. Love is not temporary, and according to 1st Corinthians 13, love bears all things. When people say "love died", I must contradict that based on the Word, and say that AGAPE was never there.

Jesus made these verses abundantly clear on the cross. He extended HIS love on the cross, to whosoever will come to HIM. When Jesus said in John

19: 30…IT IS FINISHED…IT WAS FINISHED !! Salvation and true AGAPE love was poured out for mankind. It was open and free, without respecter of persons. I could be a millionaire, or the poorest person in town. Both were on an even playing field with Jesus; both got the same love, the same plan of salvation, and the same wonderful, precious blood to wash their sins away.

The royal law of love thy neighbor as thyself, is just that…LOVE THY NEIGHBOR AS

THYSELF. I am very certain that you do not hate yourself. Therefore, you and I cannot hate others, even when others wrong us. LOVE THY NEIGHBOR AS THYSELF. When they say that you and I are everything but a child of God, Forgive and LOVE THY NEIGHBOR AS THYSELF. When you love, it cannot be, I love this one, but not that one, Love is there today, and gone tomorrow. That is NOT how Jesus treats us. Let AGAPE have its way. That is the true love of Christ !!

Today…Let us love like Jesus loves, and think like Jesus thinks, and eliminate the act of being a respecter of persons. Love is not temporary. Let us love thy neighbors as thyself, and truly please Jesus Christ today.

NINETY-ONE

29 That no flesh should glory in HIS presence.

30 But of him are ye in Christ Jesus, who of God is made unto us wisdom, and righteousness, and sanctification, and redemption:

31 That, according as it is written, He that glorieth, let him glory in the Lord.

1ˢᵗ Corinthians 1:29-31

This block of scriptures set me free whenever I read them. I them I understand that because Jesus really is so awesome, and HE is really that mighty. HE does not share HIS glory with another, and absolutely should not. When something great comes out of me, in a preaching, or a devotional...IT IS JESUS. If I lay hands on someone, and a healing takes place...IT IS JESUS. Let he that glorieth, let him glory in the LORD. While you and I meditate on the Word of God, and how our walk with Christ is going, please remember... NO FLESH SHALL GLORY IN HIS PRESENCE.

What does it mean that no flesh shall glory in HIS presence? It truly means that you and I WILL see the weaknesses and shortcomings, one of another. You and I will see another Christian fail, and commit faults before God. We will see a brother or sister have a weak moment. We will even see things go terribly wrong in the walk of a brother or sister. Please...Please...DO NOT PUT YOUR FINGER ON A BROTHER OR SISTER, WHO IS DOWN... YOUR DAY IS COMING !!

King David was a "Man After God's Own Heart". Yet, we see that King David did some terrible things, and Nathan the Prophet was sent to him, to tell him that God knew. David simply said...I have sinned against the Lord. Nathan informed David that his sin was forgiven, but there would consequences for the sin. **Do you notice that King David was NOT removed throne. So many today want a person killed off when they fall. They stub their toe, and curse, and get mad about what someone says. Some put the most abominable things on social media, and then get angry over a comment made in the bathroom. Remember Romans 3: 23...For all have sinned, and come short of the glory of God. 1st Corinthians 1:29...says no flesh shall glory in HIS presence.

When we see good that comes from us or others, let's really think about who should get the glory...it should be Jesus. If I preach well...remember that God once used a donkey to speak to Baalam the false prophet. If things do not go well, and you see it, do you ever think that the real test is on you and I...can we pray an intercede for the weak brother or sister. O how powerful the church would be if we prayed one for another, and stop gossiping about one another.

Today...Let the glory for all the good go to the LORD !! When we see the weak or the bad...quit judging...its part of our Christian life...Go into prayer for them, with Agape love in your heart...God Bless.

$\mathcal{N}$INETY-TWO

7 The fear of the Lord is the beginning of knowledge, but fools despise wisdom and instruction.

Proverbs 1: 7

5 Get wisdom, get understanding: forget it not: neither decline from the words of my mouth.

6 Forsake her not, and she shall preserve thee: love her, and she shall keep thee.

7 Wisdom is the principle thing: therefore get wisdom: and with all thy getting get understanding.

Proverbs 4: 5-7

The thing that is greatly missing in the world today, and certainly the church is wisdom. Real wisdom that is not about you and I being heady or high-minded. I am talking about a wisdom that comes from above. The kind if wisdom needed, is the kind that keeps us humble, gives us a mind to forgive. The kind of wisdom that makes a man give up racism and hatred. The wisdom needed is not earthly, but originates in the Word of God. When this kind of wisdom gets into us, the community can be changed, families reunited, and so on.

In Proverbs Chapter 1, the Word of God in Verse 7 says that the Fear of the Lord is the beginning of knowledge, but fools despise wisdom and instruction. In our hate-filled society, there is precious little wisdom from above, and a lot of thought from down- below (literally). Consider James Chapter 3, which reminds us that where there is envy, and strife in your hearts, that wisdom is called earthly, sensual, and devilish. There is an evil work attached to this way of thinking. There is no fear or respect of the Lord. Where there is no fear of the Lord, anything can be there. People openly mock God, and mistreat one another, with no fear of repercussion. That is what earthly or carnal thinking brings.

The wisdom from above is peaceable, and brings understanding. The wisdom from the Word of God is pure, it is gentle and full of mercy. This is what the church is missing. This is what families are missing. This is why children run away, families break up, domestic violence is rampant, we have so much division in our communities, and churches are in an upheaval. Because we do not operate in God's wisdom, we have strife on top of strife. We have one life mattering over another, when everyone's life is precious to Jesus (Read Ezekiel 18:4...ALL SOULS ARE MINE).

The wisdom of God comes from HIS Word, the Word of God, and HIS wisdom will keep you, and preserve you, and bring victory into your life.

Today...Walk in the wisdom of God's Word. You will have peace, and a joy unspeakable and full of glory. You will have a noticeable difference from the thinking of those around you, which will bring you great victory...God Bless.

NINETY-THREE

6 Be strong and of good courage: for unto this people shalt thou divide for an inheritance the land, which I sware unto their fathers to give them.

7 Only be thou strong and very courageous, that thou mayest to do according to all the law, which Moses my servant commanded thee: turn not from it to the right hand or to the left, that thou mayest prosper whithersoever thou goest.

10 Have not I commanded thee? Be strong and of a good courage: be not afraid, neither be thou dismayed: for the Lord thy God is with thee whithersoever thou goest.

I am speaking to someone today, who is in the trial of their life. I am in some major trials too, and I received a very powerful word to encourage me today. If we are not in proper fellowship in the house of God, getting through your trial, will be very unlikely. If I had missed service, or had a closed ear to the Lord, I would have missed the encouragement needed at this time. **The word was you were chosen to go through this battle. A lot of us are in battles and situations of our own making. We need to be honest with God, not condemn ourselves, and move to repentance. When I look at the life of King Manasseh, he had done some terrible things, and God allowed him to be jailed by the Assyrians. Once in prison, he cried unto the Lord in repentance. He was restored to the throne, and if you read Matthew Chapter one, we see that he is in the bloodline of Jesus. For whatever you have done today, repent, and watch Jesus restore you.

We are all going through trials. We all have tough situations that we are facing. Joshua was taking over for the great Moses. God had been with Moses, as he led the Children of Israel through the wilderness. They had seen the miracles of the Red Sea parting, and water coming out of a rock.

Now Moses was gone. The Children of Israel were going to face numerous enemies, who appeared stronger and greater than Israel. The Word of God was given to Joshua. Here was a great Word of strength and encouragement. He was told in Verse 6...Be strong and of good courage. Verse 7 says be strong and very courageous. In Verse 10... Be strong and of good courage...Be not afraid...be not dismayed. With all of the enemies that Joshua and Israel would face, he needed a Word of victory. So, do we!! Yes, we do have some trials of our OWN making. Revelation 3:19-20 tells us that Jesus corrects whom he loves.

There are other situations that grow us up. Romans 8:28 says this all works for our good. 1st Peter 1:7 says that the trial of our faith is more precious than gold. Then we have trials that we are chosen to go through. You can look at Job, Ezekiel, and David in the Old Testament, John, Paul, Peter, and Jesus Himself in the New Testament. Trials and Tribulations are part of our lives. We are all ordained and chosen to face certain trials, stand in Jesus through the trial, and bring Glory to His Name. Someone in despair, depressed, or maybe at the brink of suicide, needs to know that Jesus is real...AND HE WILL GET YOU THROUGH! HE said in Hebrews 13:5...I will never leave you nor forsake you.

Today...call on Jesus Name...Be strong and of good courage... God bless.

$\mathscr{N}$INETY-FOUR

2 When thou passest though the waters, I will be with thee;
and through the rivers, they shall not overflow thee: when thou
walkest through the fire, though shalt not be burned; neither shall
the flame kindle upon thee.

5 Fear not, for I am with thee: I will bring thy seed from the east,
and gather thee from the west:

Isaiah 43: 2 & 5

In Isaiah 43, we see scriptural encouragement, similar to the Word given to Joshua, when he took over for Moses. There have been numerous situations, faced by the Children of Israel and the Church of Jesus Christ. Both were going to face situations of great difficulty. Israel would face continual threats from their enemies round about them. The church would face the same challenges, but according to Jesus in Matthew 16: 18, Jesus said...I will build my church, and the gates of hell shall not prevail against it. We have a promise, that as Israel was not going to be forsaken, either is the church.

Isaiah 54: 17 tells us that... No weapon formed against shall prosper, and every tongue that shall rise against thee in judgement, thou shalt condemn. You not only have the victory over whatever situation, but also the evil voices, that would bring you to defeat. ** Yes, the weapons are going to form, BUT they will not prosper. The evil Word against us cannot prosper. You need to know today, that our enemy is defeated. Romans 8: 37 says, Nay in all these things, we are more that conquerors, through HIM that loved us. Jesus would never have given us this Word, unless we would have something to conquer. We are victorious. We are victorious, even when it does not appear that we are. Jesus was victorious, when HE said, It is finished. When HE hung HIS head on the cross and died...HE WAS VICTORIOUS!! Jesus took the keys to death, hell, and the grave on Calvary. HE was victorious, and so are we. That is why Jesus can say that the Gates of hell will not prevail. HE defeated the devil, and brought us victory.

Today...Know that you are more than a conqueror. No matter what you are going through, Jesus will be with you. HE will never leave you, nor forsake you. There may be fire, there may be a flood, but trust Jesus today...God Bless.

NINETY-FIVE

5 Peter was therefore was kept in prison: but prayer was made without ceasing of the Church of God for him.

6 And when Herod would have brought him forth, the same night Peter was sleeping between two soldiers, bound with chains: and the keepers before the door kept the prison.

7 And, behold the angel of the Lord came upon him, and a light shined in the prison: and he smote Peter on the side, and raised him up, saying, arise up quickly. And the chains fell off his hands.

There is something great about being born-again in the Church of Jesus Christ. There is something great about knowing that Jesus will hear our prayers. John 9: 31 says... And we know HE heareth not sinners; but if any man be a worshipper of God, and doeth HIS will, him HE heareth. Simon Peter was in terrible trouble. Evil King Herod had James the brother of John killed, and now he was going to kill Peter. There is one thing that you and I need to remember. When Jesus tells you something, it is going to happen. In John 21, Peter was told that he would be crucified, when he is an old man. He was a young man when this event took place. What Jesus says...WILL COME TO PASS !! Jesus says that HE will hear us when we call (Psalm 4:3). HE WILL ANSWER !!

Peter was in prison, and was going to be killed the following day. What are you up against? What situation is impossible in your life right now? I am with you, facing the impossible. How else will Jesus have people in the earth, who believe HIM for the impossible, unless there is a people, who have seen HIM do the impossible. The church needs to know that HE is the God over the impossible. **Believe me, when you are facing the impossible, there will be mocking voices, that will ridicule you for standing firm in Christ Jesus.

You have a weapon that the mocker does not have...YOU CAN PRAY, AND JESUS WILL HEAR YOU !!

When prayer went up all night, the angel came by, and woke Peter. The angel touched him, and the chains fell off. The impossible was accomplished through prayer. You and I can accomplish the impossible, when we fervently pray to the Lord in Jesus name, and believe HIM at HIS Word.

Jesus said in Luke 18:1...Men ought always to pray and not faint. ** a key to your pray breakthrough is found in Mark 11:25-26. When you stand praying... FORGIVE. When you forgive, you open heaven, and put power behind your prayer. You clear the slate, and Jesus WILL hear you.

Today...Use the most under-utilized weapon in our spiritual arsenal... Prayer. When you stand praying...Forgive. When you pray believe. Be like Peter, and watch the chains fall off...God Bless.

$\mathcal{N}$INETY-FIVE

16 For I am not ashamed of the Gospel of Christ: for it is the power of God unto salvation to everyone that believeth; to the Jew first, and also to the Greek.

Romans 1: 16

What are we ashamed of? Why are WE so sheepish about the Name of Jesus? Jesus was not ashamed of us, when HE called us HIS children. HE was proud of what HE would make of us, and boldly called us a Royal Priesthood, and a Holy Nation. Romans 5: 19 tells us that by one man's disobedience (Adam), many were made sinners, and by one man's obedience (Jesus) many were made righteous. In Hebrews 2:11, the Word of God tells us that Jesus is not ashamed to call us brothers. Why then are we ashamed of that wonderful name...JESUS.

Romans 1: 16 says that I am not ashamed of the Gospel of Christ. I have something to be proud of, and I am proud of my Saviour. HE had no problem demonstrating HIS incredible love for us, by taking OUR punishment. Jesus' love for us, that true Agape love, is something to NEVER be ashamed of. He was put open shame on the cross, uttered the words, Father, forgive them for they know not what they do. When God came to earth as a man, HE came at the time that the cruelest form of execution was in place. HE took the curse that was on man by hanging on the cross. Romans 3: 13 says cursed is everyone that hangeth on a tree. Why would I be ashamed of such a loving God, who forgave my sin, and made me new (2nd Corinthians 5:17)?

I am not ashamed of Jesus, as the Apostle Paul said the Name of Jesus is the salvation in Jesus took the anger out of me, and changed me forever. This salvation offered by Jesus, is something I am proud of, and want to tell everyone about it...Jew and Gentile...White, Black, Hispanic, or Asian... Everyone needs to know how great the redemptive power of Jesus is, and I am determined to show my gratitude, by telling the world about HIM.

Today...Show Jesus that you are not ashamed of Him. HE was not ashamed of you. Tell someone about HIM, and how great HIS salvation is...God Bless.

$\mathcal{N}$INETY-SIX

15 And he said unto them, Go, ye into all the world, and preach the gospel to every creature.

16 He that believeth and is baptized shall be saved, but he that believeth not shall be damned.

Mark 16: 15-16

13 Let us hear the conclusion of the whole matter: Fear God and keep His commandments, for this is the whole duty of man.

Ecclesiastes 12: 13

Your life has purpose!! You do not have to spend the rest of your life trying to figure out what life is all about. You don't have to spend your days contemplating your navel, and trying to find God, or a direction for your life. The Word of God has paved a clear path for you, wherein you will find peace, and great success. Jeremiah 6: 16 calls it the "Good Way" and the "Old Path".

Mark 16: 15-16 tells us of the "Great Commission", which is the direction given to us by Jesus Himself. HE gave us marching orders, that have absolute power behind them. Jesus said in Mark 16, that if you go preach the gospel in Jesus Name, sign, wonders, and miracles, and great power follow you. These great things follow YOU...WE DO NOT FOLLOW THE SIGNS.

As you read the New Testament, you see incredible things happen when people just obey the "Great Commission" and preach Jesus. Phillip saw revival in Samaria, preaching the Gospel of Jesus Christ. Peter saw the church open for the Jews and Gentiles, preaching the Gospel (Good News) of Jesus Christ. Paul saw miracle after miracle, even the dead being raised, blind eyes opening, lives changed, sin leaving the lives of men and women. How did all this happen? It all occurred by the preaching of the Gospel of Jesus Christ.

Ecclesiastes 12: 13 tells us that the whole duty of man is to fear God, and keep HIS commandments. The whole duty and life purpose of man is in the center of God's will. To move in the center of HIS will, and receive HIS blessings, HIS peace, and HIS victory; preach the Gospel of Jesus Christ. If you want a move of God for your whole family, faithfully preach the gospel. Phillip preached the Gospel in Acts Chapter 8. We then read Acts Chapter 21: 8-9, and notice that Phillip had four anointed daughters, who did prophesy. Why would Jesus bless Phillip in that manner...He preached the Gospel of Jesus Christ?

Today...walk in what the true and powerful purpose of your life. Preach the Gospel; keep HIS commandment to tell the lost world about this great and awesome salvation...God Bless.

$\mathcal{N}$INETY-SEVEN

*13 No man can serve two masters: for either he will hate the one
and love the other, and love the other. Ye cannot serve God and
Mammon.*

Luke 16: 13

8 A double minded man is unstable in all his ways.

James 1: 8

*46 And they, continuing daily with one accord in the temple,
and breaking bread from house to house, did eat their meat with
gladness and singleness of heart.*

Acts 2: 46

Are you having issues with keeping yourself stable, and spiritually on track?
How can we face the tough trials of life, with our mind and our hearts,
moving around like shifting sand? Jesus said… No man can serve two
masters. He will love the one, and despise the other. We cannot have 2 Gods.
It cannot be; Jesus today and then money tomorrow. For the early church,
as we read in Acts Chapter two, a single heart and mind, was essential
to survive. The faced persecution from their own countrymen, and the
Romans. They were also just the day to day spiritual warfare that we all
face, when we stand for Jesus and HIS righteousness. Every day I wake up,
I have to re-focus and re-commit my mind to staying on track. For Jesus…I
live, move, and have my being!!

When I purposed to serve Jesus…THE FIGHT WAS ON. Now, satan, as
the accuser of the brethren began his horrible assault. He began to move on
what is most precious to me. When you face that kind of warfare, your mind
must be made up for righteousness. The early church saw miracles, because
of an immense trust in Jesus. They were not about money and filthy lucre
today, then Jesus. They were not Mars, Jupiter, or whatever pagan god was

in today, then Jesus. HERE IS A TOUGH ONE…IT IS NOT SPOUSE, SON, OR DAUGHTER, OR FRIENDS, RELATIVES FIRST AND THEN JESUS. Jesus said in Matthew 10, He that loveth son or daughter more than me is not worthy of me. A sold-out mind for Christ, always puts HIM first. When you put HIM first, you can love others, and things, jobs, or possessions in proper balance and context. It must be that way.

James 1: 8 tells us that a double minded man is unstable in all his ways. The Children of Israel allowed double-mindedness to make a 40 day journey last 40 years. One day, they were content eating manna, and then it was time to complain, and demand Quail. You can't pray for that Prodigal in your life, and believe God today, and then declare its hopeless tomorrow. James 1: 7 even tells us that the double minded man or woman CANNOT receive anything from the LORD.

In 1st Kings 17, a confident single-minded Elijah proclaimed that it would not rain, except according to his word. He had the confidence of Deuteronomy 28th Chapter, that made it clear that if Israel rebelled, rain would not fall. When Ahab was king, Israel rebelled. A single-minded Elijah made a proclamation AND IT DID NOT RAIN FOR 3 ½ YEARS.

Today…shake off the temptation to waiver and be double-minded. Get a sold-out single, fully persuaded mind and heart, and watch Jesus move mightily in your life…God Bless.

$\mathcal{N}$INETY-EIGHT

24 Therefore whosoever heareth these sayings of mine, and doeth them, I will liken him unto a wise man, which built his house upon a rock.

25 And the rain descended and the floods came, and the winds blew, and beat upon that house; and it fell not; for it was founded upon a rock.

26 And every one that heareth these sayings of mine, and doeth them not, shall be likened unto a foolish man, which built his house upon the sand.

27 And the rain descended, and the floods came and the winds blew, and beat upon that house, and it fell, and great was the fall of it.

When you are in difficult circumstances and situations, how you respond and react really matters !! How you respond, is often simply determine, by what instruction you take in the crisis. Crisis and trouble will come to us all. If you notice in this block of scripture, Jesus makes it clear that the rain falls on all of us. The Word of God states that it rains on the just, as well as the unjust (Matthew 5:45). Since the storms will come to us all, making the Word of God the standard of how to respond is so very important. Jesus said that THE HOUSE THAT IS FOUNDED UPON THE ROCK OF HIS WORD, DOES NOT FALL. THE HOUSE FOUNDED UPON SAND FALLS, AND GREAT IS THE FALL OF IT.

When the Word of God in 1st Corinthians 13th Chapter tells us to love no matter what, that is living upon the Rock of Jesus Christ. When the 18th Chapter of Matthew tell us to forgive, always remembering that you have been forgiven, that is living on the Rock of Jesus Christ. When the Word of

God tells us to attend Church faithfully Hebrew 10:25-26), that is living on the Rock of Jesus Christ. To make it, to stand, to hold on, you need stay on the Rock of Christ Jesus. Look, I write from deep, deep experience. When the storms come...STAND ON THE ROCK OF JESUS CHRIST AND HIS UNMOVEABLE, UNCHANGEABLE WORD !!

Matthew 7 is a part of the "Sermon on the Mount". This message contains some of Jesus' greatest teaching. He, being God manifested in the flesh, knows all things that will challenge us. HE gave us all of the "Meat" needed in due season. HE, according to 2nd Peter Chapter one, gave us everything needed for life and godliness.

Today...know that the rain and storms of life are going to come, without exception. When they come (and they are coming), stand of the Rock of Christ Jesus...Stand on HIS Word, and be victorious...God bless.

$\mathcal{N}$INETY-NINE

1 He that dwelleth in the secret place of the most High, shall abide in the shadow of the Almighty.

2 I will say of the Lord, HE is my refuge and my fortress: my God; in HIM will I trust

3 Surely HE shall deliver thee from the snare of the fowler, and from the noisome pestilence.

5 Thou shalt not be afraid for the terror by night; nor for the arrow that flieth by day

14 Because he hath set HIS love upon me, therefore will I deliver him: I will be with him: I will set him on high, because he hath known my name.

It is often called the "Psalm of Protection". These Words are so important in times like these. 2nd Timothy 3 calls these times "Perilous" ...FULL OF DANGER". I survived nearly 3 decades in law enforcement. I was not the victim of a shooting or stabbing, or motor vehicle fatality. For many years, I was not living for Jesus, yet I did not meet my end. I had godly people praying for me. They interceded, and prayed that I shadow of the Almighty would rest upon me. They prayed that I would be divinely protected until the time that I would bow a knee to Jesus. When HE protects you...HE protects you !! I do not take the divine protection of Jesus for granted. I do not believe that because my vehicle spun out, and I was uninjured, that I was in right standing with God; I was not. We need to be under the protection and shadow of the almighty.

Now I have a different relationship with Jesus. I am HIS child, and am "Born again" in Jesus Christ. I surrender my will to HIM, and do my very best to follow HIS Word. I fall short, as we all do. When I do, I open the door for satan to give me a beating. So, do any of us who drop our spiritual guard. 2nd Corinthians 2:11 says we are not ignorant of satan's devices. When I put myself in a position, where I seriously need to abide in the shadow of the almighty, I turn to repentance (humble myself), prayer, and quoting the Word of God (speaking it into the situation). When you are under spiritual attack, bring Isaiah 54:17 into the situation (NO weapon that is formed against the shall prosper...). Suddenly, I find myself under the shadow of the Almighty. I find protection from the spiritual attack, that has come into the physical realm. In these perilous times, we need to know this. Jesus says we are more than a conqueror. He has put these spiritual weapons in our arsenal. When we know who we are in Jesus, we KNOW how to stay in the shadow of the Almighty.

When a child or spouse goes astray, get under the shadow of the Almighty. We can quote Acts 16:31...Believe on the Lord Jesus Christ, and thou shalt be saved; and thy house. His promise in Hebrews 7:25 says...Jesus is able to save to the uttermost. Jesus also said; all things are possible to him that believeth (Mark 9:23). Bring the situation to this Word, and you find yourself, and that family situation, under the shadow of the Almighty. HE can and will work it out !!

When you have a financial crisis, get under the shadow of the Almighty. I have done this many times. I quote Luke 6:38...Give and it shall be given to you; good measure, pressed down and shaken together, shall men give unto your bosom. I quote Malachi 3rd Chapter, and faithfully give to the Lord. Time and time again, Jesus has provided in a pinch.

Today... find yourself living in Psalm 91; the "Protection Psalm". Get under the shadow of the Almighty; surrender and trust Jesus, and watch HIM send HIS divine protection...God Bless.

29 And David said, what have I now done? Is there not a cause?

32 And David said to Saul, Let no man's heart fail thee because of him; thy servant will go and fight with this Philistine.

Some things are worth fighting for !! David was a chosen vessel for the Lord. He was chosen to be king over Israel instead of the rebellious Saul. He was the least of his brothers, and not regarded highly. He was at home watching the sheep, while his older brothers went to war with the Philistines. The army of Israel was challenged day after day by Goliath. He was 9 feet tall. He was a man of war. Saul was King of Israel and was 7 feet tall. It was Saul's job to fight Goliath. He had rebelled against God, and the anointing of God had departed from him. He would not carry out the assignment that he was chosen for.

Then there was David. When Goliath came out and mocked God, David became angry, to the core of his being. Why? Because the Anointing of God was upon him. David loved God. If we love God, when someone mocks HIM, it troubles us. Galatians 6 reminds us that…God is not mocked. David had a cause. We NEED to have a cause. We need to have things in our lives that matter. We need to stand for SOMETHING!! If you do not stand for SOMETHING…you will fall for ANYTHING !! The things that pertain to Jesus, truly need to matter. Holiness (Heb 12:14), Forgiveness (Mark 11:25-26), Salvation (John 3:1-7); all need to matter. Evangelism, and telling people about Jesus; needs to matter (Mark 16:15-18). IS THERE NOT A CAUSE??

The early church were persecuted by Nero, who was emperor of Rome. He fed Christians to the lions, and lit many of the early brethren on fire; just because they loved and worshipped Jesus. ** Many of us have suffered and faced terrible situations, because we have made a stand for Christ. Maybe we have not faced the degree of persecution that they faced in the first century, but many of us have suffered loss for the cause of Christ. IS THERE NOT A CAUSE??

David made the stand to face Goliath, even if it led to his death or destruction. There was a cause, worth putting his life on the line. Trust me; there are things worth taking a stand for…JESUS and HIS word, and HIS Agape love. When David chose to stand against Goliath, and put his trust totally in God, his victory was assured. The Power of God came upon him, and through God's anointing. He slew Goliath, and became God's champion. He got into the flow of the Spirit of God, and found a place of victory.

Today…IS THERE NOT AS CAUSE?? Take a stand for Jesus Christ today. Be a David, and allow the glory of God to move in you. HE will bring you, your family or church great victory…God Bless.

$\mathcal{O}$NE HUNDRED ONE

1 Now faith is the substance of things hoped for; the evidence of things not seen.

6 But without faith, it is impossible to please him; for he that cometh to God must believe that He is, and He is the rewarder of them that diligently seek Him.

Hebrews 11:1&6

34 And he said unto her, Daughter, thy faith hath made thee whole; go in peace, and be whole of thy plague.

Mark 5:34

A woman had an issue, and had a very serious need. She had a physical plague, and had spent all that she had, seeking the doctors for a healing. She saw Jesus walking toward the house of Jairus, who was a religious leader. When the woman touched the hem of Jesus garment, she was instantly healed. ** Let me say plainly, that I am not speaking against doctors or the medical community. I was healed of cancer in 2009. I give Jesus 100% of the glory. It was Jesus, who had me ask my doctor for a PSA test, literally as I was walking out of his office. It was Jesus, who led me to my Oncologist. My doctor was treating a young man, who died of a very aggressive form of cancer. I asked the doctor if I could pray for him. He said that he really wanted all of us who were assembled there to pray for him. We prayed for him, and I was impressed by his humbleness. **When I found that I had cancer (by Jesus' mercy), I called the same doctor. He set up a treatment course of radiation. I was healed completely of prostate cancer, and my PSA is at zero.

I wanted to establish my position about the medical community, and express my love and respect for them. **It is always important, however to give Jesus the glory for the healing. HIS hand is there when medication, or a course of treatment works. The woman with the issue of blood touched them hem of Jesus' garment. She was instantly healed of her affliction. She demonstrated great faith by touching the hem of Jesus' garment. The affliction was instantly removed from her body. Please note: Jesus referred to her as daughter! She sought the Lord by faith, and according to Hebrews 11:6, she diligently sought the Lord. Jesus rewarded her for her faith, healed her, and called her "Daughter". She demonstrated the substance of things hoped for; Jesus met her there and healed her completely. HE is truly waiting for us to come to HIM by faith and trust. HE said; Thy faith has made thee whole.

Today...Jesus is waiting for us to come to HIM by faith. He is waiting; just waiting for the opportunity to call us son or daughter, and do miracles in our lives...God Bless.

⟨O⟩NE HUNDRED TWO

13 But I would not have you to be ignorant brethren, concerning them which are asleep, that ye sorrow not, even as others which have no hope.

14 For if we believe that Jesus died and rose again, even so them which sleep in Jesus, will God bring with him.

16 For the Lord himself shall descend from heaven with a shout, with the voice of the archangel, and with the trump of God, and the dead in Christ shall rise first.

17 Then we which are alive and remain shall be caught up together with them in the clouds to meet the lord in the air, and so shall we ever be with the Lord.

1ˢᵗ Thessalonians 4: 13-14 & 16-17

This event is recorded in Matthew 24, Mark 13, Luke 21, 1ˢᵗ Thessalonians 4, 1ˢᵗ Corinthians 15, and is consistent theme in the Book of Revelation. The event is called the "Rapture" or "Catching Away" of the church. There is all of this New Testament scripture reminding us again and again, that Jesus is coming back, and HE will gather His church, and bring us to glory with HIM. HE has been working on our new residence for over 2000 years. Jesus made this beautiful world in 6 days. HE has been working on our heavenly home for 2000 years. Can you imagine how awesome it will be?

Jesus HIMSELF ascended to heaven in Acts Chapter one. This was not done in a closet. HIS ascension was done in front of approximately 500 witnesses. In Acts 1: 9, it is recorded that Jesus was taken up to heaven on a cloud, and will return in like manner. The Word of God also gives us additional pictures of the "Catching Away" of the church. In Genesis 5:24; the scripture records this event. The word of God says that God took Enoch, and he went alive to heaven. In 2nd Kings 2:11, the Chariots of Fire descended from heaven, and took Elijah alive to heaven; he was caught away. In Matthew 17, we later see Elijah and Moses having a conversation on the Mount of Transfiguration, with Jesus HIMSELF.

There is just way too much scriptural evidence that this event is going to take place. The "Rapture" or "Catching Away" of the church is GOING TO HAPPEN!! The dead in Christ will rise first; yes, the graves will open. Revelation 20 says that the sea will give up the dead. Matthew 24 tells us that two will be working in the field; one will be taken, and the other left. 1st Corinthians 15: 50-58 tells us that this change; corruption must put on incorruption; will take place, in a moment, in the twinkling of an eye.

Since it is clear that Jesus will return to bring HIS bride, the church with HIM, and it will happen soon, we need to make sure that we are in the number who will be caught up. Jesus have us a picture of a sheep, who will be taken, and a goat that will be left behind. He gave us the picture of 5 wise virgins in Matthew 25, and 5 foolish virgins. He likened the 5 foolish virgins, to those who wanted to get into a marriage feast, but it was too late; the door was shut. Noah's Ark is another picture of this time. When the door of the Ark was shut, it was too late for those who missed out. The doors were shut, and they could not get in. ** You must be "Born-Again" in Jesus to get in. You must be baptized. You must be "Born-again" of the water and the Spirit. This is NOT my opinion...These are Jesus 'exact words in John 3:1-7. HE said it; I am only echoing what the King of Kings told us. ** We must repent, and turn away from sin. We must forgive everybody for everything (Mark 11:25-26). We must fulfill the Great Commission, and preach the gospel to every creature.

Today...Know that Jesus loves us very much (real Agape love), and is coming back to get us. Let us work and strive to be ready today, for this great event is coming soon...God Bless.

$\mathcal{O}$NE HUNDRED THREE

21 Not every one that saith unto me, Lord, Lord, shall enter into the kingdom of heaven; but he that doeth the will of my father, which is in heaven.

22 Many will say in that day Lord, lord, have we nor prophesied in thy name? and in thy name hath cast out devils? And in thy name done many wonderful works?

23 And then I will profess unto them, I never knew you, I never knew you: depart from me ye that work iniquity

These three verses always make me think, and do what 1st and 2nd Corinthians remind us to do...LET A MAN EXAMINE HIMSELF. Jesus makes it clear in these verses in Matthew that there will be men and women, who come before HIM, and be surprised that they will be turned away in judgement. ** There is absolutely no need or this to happen to any of us !! The people who are turned away by Jesus, are people who are Christians. The scriptures remind us that these people say to Jesus...LORD. They question, and say Lord didn't I prophesy in your name. or cast out devils in your name? Jesus will say to them...Depart ye that work iniquity; I never knew you.

The iniquity is the inner darkness of the heart. The iniquity is the unforgiveness, that we hide way down inside. We conceal the bitterness against someone else, and just go on daily saying...Jesus could not possibly know how much I really don't like brother or sister so and so. Please remember what Ecclesiastes 12:14 says; for God shall bring every work into judgement, with every secret thing, whether ii be good, or whether it be evil. Jesus has an x-ray eye. HE knows all things. I can even put on a smile with my brother or sister, and have thoughts of evil toward them. Jesus knows the thoughts. Jesus knew the thoughts of HIS disciples. HE said that HE chose twelve, and one is a devil. HE knew the thoughts of Judas. HE knew the thoughts of the Pharisees, when they judged HIM, and the woman washed his feet, weeping, with her hair. Jesus knows all things, and said DEPART, to those who will not forgive; DEPART for those who hate, DEPART for the racist heart, DEPART for the heart of bitterness.

I never want to hear Jesus tell me to depart. I always want to check myself, and examine myself. Jesus has caught me many times with a little bit of darkness inside, that HE saw, and I did not even know was there. It was the little hidden things, way down dep inside.

I had a sign up in my cubicle at work...DO YOU WANT TO HEAR WELL DONE, OR BE WELL DONE !! That sign was to remind me to continually examine myself, and check my inward thoughts.

Today...Please check yourself; get rid of all bitterness, evil thoughts in your heart, and unforgiveness. Work today to have a heart of love; true Agape love, and mercy...God Bless.

ⓞNE HUNDRED FOUR

7 So when they continued asking him, he lifted up himself and said unto them, He that is without sin among you, let him first cast a stone at her.

John 8:7

In closing this first devotional book, there must be a reminder to me and to you. Jesus response to the accusers of the woman caught in adultery; He that is without sin among you, let him first cast a stone at her. Romans 3:23 is like a brick wall in front of us. It says that ALL have sinned, and come short of the glory of God. ALL really does mean ALL. We love to think and talk about the sin of others. It is easy to turn on the news, and see the weaknesses of others. People today relish in the fall of a politician, preacher or public official. It is an unfortunate church and societal reality…talk about everyone else's failures. ** I would ask another question; How many days have you prayed and fasted for that weak person? Why do I ask that question? Because, AGAPE love tells me to pray for my weak brother or sister; do not spend time judging them. Praying and fasting and interceding for a struggling brother or sister is what Jesus would have us to do. ** What HE does not want us to do is to pick up a rock, forget our own sin, and kill off a weaker saint.

Romans 15: 1 tells us that We that are strong, ought to bear the infirmities of the weak, and not to please ourselves. ** If I am having a weak moment, please do not pick up a judgement stone, to hurl at me when I am down. Remember, your day is coming!! We all have sinful, and often embarrassing moments. If you pick up the stone, remember Jesus' Words… Let he who is without sin cast the first stone at her. Who can cast a stone…No one? By the way, if you say in your heart, they should know better; this may be true, but then there is Jesus checking the iniquity of our very own hearts.

Agape love tells me NOT to pick up the stone, when Jesus made a stipulation… Let he who is without sin cast the stone. NONE OF US SHOULD EVER GO

NEAR THE ROCK PILE, BUT GET TO KNEES, AND PRAY FOR THE WEAK. Jesus said that there were none there to condemn the woman. As much as HE told her to go and sin no more, HE gives all of us that same charge. So often, the sin we commit, is putting our fingers on others.

Today…and always; Let us remember that when we point the finger at other, there three fingers pointed right back at us. Stay away from the rock pile. We have all sinned; let us remember that our job is to pray for the weak, love and restore them…God Bless.

$\mathscr{A}$BOUT THE AUTHOR

Dr. Victor A. Kennedy, Ph.D. (Doctor of Theology), serves as one of the pastors in the Assemblies of Jesus Christ Ministries. He has been a member and minister there for nearly 25 years. He spent 11 years conducting weekly services at the Juvenile Detention Center in Rockville, Maryland, while serving as a police officer, and detective with the Montgomery County, Maryland Police Department. He served on the Montgomery County Police  Department for 29 years, and retired in 2012. He was an investigator for 18 years in the Family Crimes Division-Missing Children's Section, and handled over 8000 missing children cases. In 2013, Dr. Kennedy started a new life chapter, and now serves as a Case Manager 2 at the National Center for Missing and Exploited Children in Alexandria, Virginia. He views his role in locating missing children as a direct parallel to his ministry; finding and recovering the lost.

Dr. Kennedy was privileged to represent the United States in international powerlifting competition. He was a 3-time Drug-Free National Powerlifting Champion (1989, 1991, 1992). He is a former American Record holder in the squat at 944 pounds. He often uses the challenges of lifting heavy weights, to illustrate spiritual lessons of life. In other words; No pain...No gain, or "You can't quit halfway through the lift".

Dr. Kennedy began sending out devotional text messages in 2015, as an encouragement to some of the church members. The 10 to 15 weekly recipients, quickly grew to over 100, and not long after, to over 200. The text message devotional ministry, opened the door for him to write this devotional book, "Meat in Due Season". He stresses the main tenants of Jesus Christ's amazing love and forgiveness for us. He frequently makes the point to forgive everyone for everything. The benchmark scripture that Dr. Kennedy weaves into his personal life, and writing is Mark 11:25-26, where Jesus says, if we do not forgive, we are not forgiven. Dr. Kennedy makes this a clear theme in his writing, teaching, and preaching.

He is a lifelong Maryland resident, and sincerely desires that all readers are strengthened and encouraged by this book.

Printed in the United States
By Bookmasters